TEACHING *with* digital images

ACQUIRE · ANALYZE · CREATE · COMMUNICATE

GLEN L. BULL

LYNN BELL

EDITORS

International Society for Technology in Education

EUGENE, OREGON · WASHINGTON, DC

TEACHING *with* digital images

ACQUIRE · ANALYZE · CREATE · COMMUNICATE

Glen L. Bull and Lynn Bell, Editors

DIRECTOR OF PUBLISHING
Jean Marie Hall

COPY EDITOR
Lynne Ertle

ACQUISITIONS EDITOR
Scott Harter

BOOK DESIGN
Kim McGovern

PRODUCTION EDITOR
Tracy Cozzens

COVER DESIGN
Kim McGovern

PRODUCTION COORDINATOR
Amy Miller

LAYOUT AND PRODUCTION
Tracy Cozzens

International Society for Technology in Education (ISTE)
Washington, DC, Office: 1710 Rhode Island Ave. NW, Suite 900, Washington, DC 20036
Eugene, Oregon, Office: 175 West Broadway, Suite 300, Eugene, OR 97401-3003
Order Desk: 1.800.336.5191
Order Fax: 1.541.302.3778
Customer Service: orders@iste.org
Books and Courseware: books@iste.org
Rights and Permissions: permissions@iste.org
Web site: www.iste.org

First Edition
ISBN 10: 1-56484-219-3
ISBN 13: 978-1-56484-219-0

About ISTE

THE INTERNATIONAL Society for Technology in Education (ISTE) is a nonprofit professional organization with a worldwide membership of leaders in educational technology. We are dedicated to promoting appropriate uses of technology to support and improve learning, teaching, and administration in PK–12 education and teacher education. As part of that mission, ISTE provides high-quality and timely information, services, and materials, such as this book.

ISTE Book Publishing works with experienced educators to develop and produce practical resources for classroom teachers, teacher educators, and technology leaders. Every manuscript we select for publication is carefully peer reviewed and professionally edited. We look for content that emphasizes the effective use of technology where it can make a difference—increasing the productivity of teachers and administrators; helping students with unique learning styles, abilities, or backgrounds; collecting and using data for decision making at the school and district levels; and creating dynamic, project-based learning environments that engage 21st-century learners. We value your feedback on this book and other ISTE products. E-mail us at **books@iste.org**.

ISTE is home of the National Educational Technology Standards (NETS) Project, the National Educational Computing Conference (NECC), and the National Center for Preparing Tomorrow's Teachers to Use Technology (NCPT[3]). To learn more about these and other ISTE initiatives and to view our complete book list or request a print catalog, visit our Web site at **www.iste.org**. **You'll find information about:**

- ISTE, our mission and our members

- Membership opportunities and services

- Online communities and special interest groups (SIGs)

- Professional development services

- Research and evaluation services

- Educator resources

- ISTE's National Educational Technology Standards (NETS) for Students, Teachers and Administrators

- *Learning & Leading with Technology* magazine

- *Journal of Research on Technology in Education*

About the Editors

 GLEN L. BULL is the Ward Professor of Education in the Curry School of Education at the University of Virginia and is editor of *Contemporary Issues in Technology and Teacher Education* (www. CITEjournal.org). He previously served as director of Teacher-LINK, one of the nation's first regional K-12 Internet systems, and developed one of the nation's first statewide K-12 Internet systems, Virginia's Public Education Network. He is also a past president of the Virginia Society for Technology in Education. Nationally, he is a founding member and past president of the Society for Information Technology and Teacher Education. In 2000 he became the second recipient of the society's Willis Award for Outstanding Lifetime Achievement in Technology and Teacher Education.

 LYNN BELL works with the Center for Technology and Teacher Education at the University of Virginia. She has worked as managing editor of the online journal *Contemporary Issues in Technology and Teacher Education* since its inception in 2000 and is now a co-editor of the journal with Glen L. Bull. In addition, for the past eight years she has served as technical editor for the journal *School Science and Mathematics.*

About the Authors

RANDY L. BELL is a science educator with 18 years of experience teaching science and technology courses at the secondary and post-secondary levels. Randy is currently an associate professor in the Curry School of Education at the University of Virginia, where he teaches secondary science methods, technology integration, and research methods and serves as a fellow with the Center for Technology and Teacher Education. He has published a number of papers in both research and practitioner publications, and he co-edited the ISTE book *NETS·S Curriculum Series: Science Units for Grades 9-12* with Joe Garofalo.

MICHAEL J. BERSON is an associate professor in the Secondary Education Department at the University of South Florida. He instructs courses in social science methodology and is a coordinator of the doctoral studies program in social science education. His courses have been nationally recognized for integrating emerging technologies into instruction and modeling dynamic and fluid pedagogy. He is currently a vice president of the Society for Information Technology and Teacher Education. He has extensively published books, chapters, and journal articles and presented worldwide.

BARBARA CHAMBERLIN is the extension instructional design and educational media specialist at New Mexico State University. She integrates digital photography into the curriculum of informal educational settings, such as 4-H. Her other areas of academic interest include digital video in education and the development of educational computer games. In her position, she helps incorporate technology into instruction and outreach activities and leads the Learning Games Lab. Her doctorate is in instructional technology from the University of Virginia.

JOE GAROFALO is co-director of the Center for Technology and Teacher Education and associate professor of mathematics education. He teaches courses in secondary mathematics pedagogy, problem solving, and mathematics education research, and coordinates the five-year BA/MT secondary mathematics teacher education program at the Curry School. Joe's interests in mathematics education include mathematical problem solving, use of technology in mathematics teaching, and mathematics teacher education. He co-edited the ISTE book *NETS·S Curriculum Series: Science Units for Grades 9-12* with Randy L. Bell.

TOM HAMMOND is a fellow at the Center for Technology and Teacher Education in the Curry School of Education at the University of Virginia. He taught secondary history, economics, English, and computer programming for 10 years, both in the United States and abroad.

SARA B. KAJDER is an assistant professor of literacy education at the University of Louisville. A former graduate fellow in English education at the Center for Technology and Teacher Education at the University of Virginia, she also taught middle and high school English in Montgomery County, Maryland. She was the recipient of the 2002 Conference on English Education National Technology Leadership Fellowship. She is the author of *The Tech Savvy English Classroom.*

ELIZABETH LANGRAN has been teaching French, social studies, and English as a second language since 1992, both in the U.S. and overseas in Morocco and Switzerland. She is a doctoral student in instructional technology at the University of Virginia, and a fellow for the Center for Technology and Teacher Education. Elizabeth holds the position of director of the Technology Infusion Program, a partnership between the Curry School of Education and the Albemarle County School District. In 2005 she received the Outstanding Graduate Teaching Assistant award, and the Faculty Senate Dissertation Year Fellowship to pursue her research in technology and leadership, to be completed in spring 2006.

JOHN C. PARK is an associate professor of science education at North Carolina State University, where he earned the title of Alumni Distinguished Undergraduate Professor for exemplary teaching. His research interests focus on the use of images in science instruction, including Web-based instruction, microcomputer-based laboratories, and digital video. He is the owner of Science Junction, one of the earliest Web sites devoted to Science Education, which debuted in 1997 (**www.ncsu.edu/ sciencejunction/**). From its genesis, the site focused on the use of images to promote a science community for teachers and students.

RICHARD SEBASTIAN attended Virginia Commonwealth University and earned a bachelor's degree in English with a minor in religious studies. He worked in the field of adult education for several years, teaching G.E.D. courses, computer classes, and employment skills for Henrico County. He also became involved in the local independent film scene in Richmond, Virginia, producing several film shorts. Richard is a doctoral student in instructional technology in the University of Virginia's Curry School of Education, where he teaches courses on computer technology skills and digital multimedia development. His research interests are in the areas of educational gaming and collaborative learning.

BRIAN SHARP is an assistant professor of mathematics at Indiana University of Pennsylvania. Brian first became interested in using digital imagery in the mathematics classroom in the mid-1990s, when he was a high school mathematics teacher in rural Virginia. There, he used digital images to add excitement and real-world connections to his classroom. His students worked with digital images to determine heights of flagpoles, approximate the slope of rooftops of houses being built by vocational students, and to calculate the "spread" of a locally famous white-tail deer known as the "Milboro Monster."

JULIE SPRINGER is an art historian and educator who specializes in modern art and women's history. As the coordinator of teacher programs at the National Gallery of Art in Washington, D.C., she is responsible for developing workshops and teaching materials that make the gallery's collections accessible to educators nationwide. She is responsible for the gallery's annual Teacher Institute, which has encouraged understanding of the visual arts through digital technologies. Prior to coming to Washington, Julie was the curator of American painting at the Georgia Museum of Art at the University of Georgia, Athens. She is a regular contributor to the *Woman's Art Journal*.

KATHLEEN OWINGS SWAN is an assistant professor at the University of Kentucky. Her research interests include examining strategies for training preservice and inservice social studies teachers to effectively use educational technology in social studies instruction. She is the 2005 recipient of the National Technology Leadership Initiative award presented by the Society for Information Technology and Teacher Education on behalf of the NCSS College and University Faculty Assembly.

ANN THOMPSON, a former high school mathematics teacher, is a professor at Iowa State University and the founding director of the Center for Technology in Learning and Teaching. She is past president of the Society for Information Technology in Teacher Education and the editor of the ISTE publication the *Journal of Computing in Teacher Education*. She serves as a consultant in the area of technology in teacher education to colleges and universities. She was recently named to the Iowa Academy of Education and given the title of University Professor.

Contents

PART 2 ■ Using Digital Images across the Curriculum

PART 1

learning to work with
digital images

CHAPTER 1

Glen L. Bull and Lynn Bell

incorporating digital images in instruction

MANY SCHOOL subjects can best be learned and understood through visual imagery. Maps in geography, microscopic images in biology, star fields in astronomy, photos of contemporary and historical events in social studies, and graphical images in mathematics are some of the common uses of visual images that immediately come to mind.

Many students also have a visual learning style. Some of these students may have difficulty understanding new information if it is presented only verbally. It has long been acknowledged that multiple representations of new concepts—verbal, graphic, and numeric—can facilitate understanding by all students and can be particularly useful for visual learners.

Until recently, the resources for incorporating images into classroom teaching have been limited to low-resolution overhead transparencies and slide projection machines. Three digital revolutions, however, have occurred in close proximity and forever changed these circumstances. The first was the advent of the World Wide Web. In little more than a decade, the Web has become an essential medium for information, entertainment, and commerce, making its adoption by society even faster than television before it. Many U.S. classrooms have been connected to the Internet in the same short time span. Formerly, science students might have had access to only a few dozen images in a printed textbook; now, thanks to the Web, they have access to tens of thousands of images illustrating almost every conceivable topic.

During the same time, a revolution in camera technology took place. At the start of the 21st century, for the first time, more digital cameras were sold than film cameras in the U.S. A majority of American families now own at least one digital camera. With digital cameras appearing in everything from cell phones to handheld computers to personal media players, they are among the most ubiquitous technologies around. This represents a significant opportunity for schools. Digital cameras can be used to facilitate the instructional use of images in ways that previously could be accomplished only with great difficulty or expense. Digital cameras can also make it practical to address curricular objectives that were heretofore not achievable at all. Digital image technology allows students to acquire their own images or use images viewed on the Web, modifying them as needed to fulfill particular project requirements.

Currently, we are in the midst of a third revolution: the transition from analog to digital display technologies. As a result, compact, inexpensive projection systems are now readily available and are being acquired for classrooms in record numbers. This advance is important because it allows an entire class of students to view a single computer display.

Why This Book?

MANY TEACHERS and technology coordinators are already using digital cameras to record student activities and communicate classroom events. These uses are quite valuable and make it possible to include images of student activities in newsletters sent to parents or to document steps in a science experiment for a class Web site.

However, the focus of this book is different. This book explores using digital images to help students learn content in ways that would have been difficult or impossible without this technology. For example, the ability to display an image of an amoeba swimming under a digital microscope can change how science teachers structure particular lessons. The goal of this book is to explore innovative teaching methods using digital images in science, language arts, mathematics, and social studies.

In speaking of digital images, we are referring to both still images and video. Many still digital cameras can now capture short video clips, and digital video cameras can capture still images. Digital software such as iMovie and Movie Maker (now standard components of the Macintosh and Windows operating systems, respectively) can be used to create digital movies from a montage of still images. Thanks to the versatility of the digital medium, formerly separate capabilities are now merging to offer new possibilities.

This book begins with a few chapters on digital photography basics—how to take digital photos or acquire them from other sources, how to choose and use the image editing software needed to manipulate, display, and publish the images, and what you need to know about copyright issues and the fair use of digital photographs found on the Web. However, the focus of this book is less on the "how?" than it is on the "why?": why should teachers in all content areas consider using digital images to teach their subjects? The meat of this book, therefore, comes in part 2, where we discuss the instructional uses of digital images in the core curriculum areas.

Electronic files of most of the images in this book are provided on the accompanying CD-ROM for use in the classroom. The CD also offers a host of links to online resources that will help you take advantage of the wealth of material and how-to information available on the Internet.

Digital Images in the Curriculum

AN OVERVIEW of the ways that digital images are being used in the different subject areas is outlined below, with in-depth descriptions provided in the corresponding chapters in part 2.

SCIENCE

Digital images can be applied in a number of useful ways in science classrooms. Visualization tools can help students observe events that are either too small (biological microorganisms), too fast (the trajectory of a dropped ball in a physics or math classroom), or too slow (the transformation of a caterpiller into a chrysalis) to see otherwise (Figure 1). These uses can be facilitated by adapters that allow digital cameras to be attached to microscopes for biological observations, or to telescopes for astronomical observations.

Many standard digital cameras are capable of capturing a time-lapse series of photographs that would have previously required complicated, expensive equipment. The "Life in a Bird's Nest" and "Metamorphosis of a Butterfly" activities described in the science chapter are examples of this type of classroom use. Digital images are also useful for exploring topographic maps in Earth science and for analyzing the motion of a toy car in physics. Chapter 6 describes these and similar activities and provides practical tips for undertaking them in the science classroom.

FIGURE 1. Photography is a great addition to the science curriculum.

LANGUAGE ARTS

Good readers often visualize the action of a story they are reading, creating internal mental images that help them make sense of the action and remember its details. Struggling readers, on the other hand, often lack this capacity. The chapter on digital images in the language arts classroom (chapter 7) provides ideas and examples for bridging this gap through a variety of activities that encourage readers to envision text. These strategies range from the use of images in visual think alouds to digital storytelling, a new form of narrative that builds upon time-honored oral traditions. Descriptions of ways to implement these strategies are provided, based on extensive classroom experience with digital image technology.

MATHEMATICS

Students who struggle to master reading and writing can still see the relevance of the skills they are learning to their everyday life. This is not always the case for math students who struggle to master the symbols and procedures of arcane formulas and equations. Mathematics employs a unique symbol system that often remains a distant abstraction even for adults.

Images offer one of the more effective ways of establishing a connection between these abstract mathematical symbols and the world around us. Images acquired with a digital camera can be imported into the computer for analysis. This analysis can be accomplished informally in the early grades through easy-to-use image editors that facilitate explorations of drawings and perspective, or more formally through the use of specialized tools such as the Geometer's Sketchpad.

Digital imaging technologies also provide ways to bring the static images in math textbooks to life. Digital cameras and computers allow exploration of three-dimensional objects over time. Ideas for employing such activities are outlined in the mathematics chapter (chapter 8).

SOCIAL STUDIES

The relevance of digital images to social studies is readily apparent. Repositories of digital images in sites such as the Virginia Center for Digital History allow students to directly access and interpret primary source material in much the same way a historian might. Faculty members of many university history departments have incorporated these resources into their teaching methods, and the practice is spreading to K–12 schools as well.

Many classes are now moving beyond the use of these digital repositories to undertake projects that actively capture and record community history in electronic portfolios. In some instances, these projects are conducted in collaboration with scholars who serve as advisors and consultants. While community history projects have been around for a long time (preserving information that otherwise would be lost), new digital tools facilitate this process. Such projects are described in the chapter on digital images in social studies (chapter 9).

A Framework for Using Digital Images

THE WAYS digital images can be used differ from subject to subject—from capturing images of microscopic organisms in the science classroom to examining primary digital sources in the history classroom. All of these uses, however, have certain elements in common. All of the activities described in the content area chapters involve one or more of the following phases:

- *acquire* images

- *analyze* images

- *create* image-based works

- *communicate* ideas and understandings

These four phases—acquire, analyze, create, and communicate—do not necessarily occur in a linear sequence (nor is the order in which they are presented here intended to suggest this). Rather, activities involving images may begin at any phase and often will cycle back and forth among different phases in an iterative fashion (see Figure 2).

ACQUIRE

The explosion of new imaging technologies now offers students many opportunities to participate in the acquisition and selection of images. Science students can use digital cameras to acquire images of leaves for digital leaf collections. Students in social studies classes can use digital cameras to acquire images for inclusion in community histories. Search engines on the Web can unearth a plethora of images on almost any topic.

FIGURE 2. Activities involving digital images in the classroom may begin and end at any phase: acquire, analyze, create, and communicate.

ANALYZE

Using images in the classroom can involve many kinds of analysis. The development of a classification system for a digital leaf collection requires one type of analysis. Software such as the Geometer's Sketchpad can be used to analyze images of natural objects or architectural structures for the presence of ratios such as the golden rectangle. Social studies students learn that selecting images that tell the story of a community involves analysis of historical events and communal values.

CREATE

Educational activities often involve the creation of products. In the past, these works have typically consisted of written words on a page. However, today's word processing software makes incorporating images both possible and easy. This capability allows math students, for example, to incorporate multiple representations of a particular mathematic concept in their reports—numeric, algebraic, graphical, and pictorial.

Products need not be limited to printed documents. Students in language arts classes can use images to develop digital stories that have great impact. Similarly, students in social studies classes can employ the same methods that the director Ken Burns has used to develop historical documentaries of community events.

COMMUNICATE

The ultimate objective of nearly all social endeavors is to communicate. Today, electronic portfolios, blogs (short for Web logs), and class Web sites facilitate the communication of student learning to teachers and the community at large. A paper or product that was formerly read only by a teacher can now be communicated to a larger audience.

An electronic medium makes it possible and easy to share student products, such as a digital story in language arts, a historical narrative in social studies, or a digital movie of an experiment in science. The National Council of Teachers of English is in the midst of a conversation about "multimodal writing." Acts of authorship that go beyond text are likely to become a requisite for literacy in the future.

The selection and sequence of images from a historical database can become an element of a rubric used to assess historical understanding. Similarly, the manner in which a digital story is constructed can provide a basis for assessment in language arts. The first generation of teachers engaged in this type of authorship in schools is currently working out the principles for using these works to assess student learning and understanding.

In some instances, activities and products might be shared only with other students in the class. Electronic collaboration tools, for example, now facilitate peer review in English class. In other cases, products can be shared with other classes in geographically distant sites. The Internet also makes it possible to share these products with parents. Digital documents and Web sites make it just as easy to share images as it is to share words.

Increasingly, electronic portfolios are being employed to capture and assess student learning. The electronic medium facilitates the incorporation of both still and moving images into the assessment process, providing a record of achievement over time.

The ISTE NETS for Students

THE ISTE National Educational Technology Standards for Students (NETS·S) provide a useful context for thinking about digital images in the curriculum. Each of the four phases in the digital imaging instructional framework has parallels in the NETS·S (see Table 1).

Acquire. The myriad search engines for digital images—such as the Google image search feature—now facilitate identification and acquisition of figures, illustrations, and pictures as well as text. This corresponds well with NETS·S Item 5, which recommends that students be taught to use technology to locate and acquire information.

Analyze. Similarly, the analysis phase finds parallels in NETS·S Item 6, which recommends that students be capable of using technological resources for making informed decisions. Visual representations can make important contributions to informed decision-making.

Create. The create phase finds a correspondence in NETS·S Item 3, which recommends that technology tools be employed to produce models, publications, and creative works.

TABLE 1. Digital Images and the NETS for Students

PHASE		NETS·S
ACQUIRE	5	Students use technology to locate, evaluate, and collect information from a variety of sources.
ANALYZE	6	Students use technology resources for solving problems and making informed decisions.
CREATE	3	Students use productivity tools to collaborate in constructing technology-enhanced models, preparing publications, and producing other creative works.
COMMUNICATE	4	Students use a variety of media and formats to communicate information and ideas effectively to multiple audiences.

The capability for incorporating images into reports and papers is one of the more compelling reasons behind the shift from traditional handwritten or typed assignments to word processing.

Communicate. A new class of collaborative software is now emerging and transforming business, entertainment, and social life, ranging from blogs to wikis (collaborative Web sites). This phase is recognized in NETS·S Item 4, which recommends that students be taught to use a variety of media to communicate effectively. The images that are embedded in digital stories, historical narratives, and digital movies of scientific experiments are a new media class. Images can be incorporated into any Web log, but a new class of blogs focusing on images, known as "photoblogs," is now emerging. With appropriate guidance from teachers, these new and emerging capabilities can easily be employed for effective communication.

Categories of Use

SOME USES of digital imagery in the classroom could also be implemented with traditional film cameras. However, digital images amplify and extend these uses. For example, a digital image can be incorporated into a word processing document, saved in an electronic portfolio, or posted on the Web. There are also substantial benefits in convenience and cost. Digital images can be used at once, without waiting for film to be processed and returned. Students can preview digital images and retake pictures immediately if necessary. Digital cameras also allow students to take more pictures and experiment with lighting, focus, framing, and composition in ways that would be prohibitively expensive with a film camera.

The cost savings can be instructionally significant. In the 1970s, the Polaroid Corporation distributed free cameras to selected teachers for educational use. In many cases, once the package of film provided with the educational kit was used, the cameras were placed on the shelf and left to gather dust. Teachers simply lacked the funds needed to purchase additional film. Similarly, scientists have used time-lapse photography to study natural phenomena since the 19th century. However, cost and technical difficulty were significant obstacles to incorporating these methods in science classes prior to the advent of digital cameras.

Table 2 presents an overview of ways that digital images can be appropriately used in the four core content areas. These categories of use have emerged through discussion and are intended to be illustrative rather than comprehensive.

Digital Images and Emerging Technology

RECENTLY WE have seen an explosion of social and collaborative software designed to bring groups of people together to interact and communicate. The ubiquitous presence of digital cameras in cell phones, PDAs, wireless and wired Web cams, and many other formats has changed how people use images. In the past, pictures were often collected in photo albums and shoeboxes and were seldom viewed except on special occasions. Digital images, however, can be transmitted electronically. This has given rise to imaging sharing sites such as Flikr (**www.flikr.com**) that represent yet another type of social experiment in human collaboration. Flikr accounts are available to anyone without charge, and allow photographs to be tagged and shared.

The new practice of collaborative categorization using freely chosen keywords known as *folksonomy* (i.e., folk's taxonomy) is also gaining in popularity. These collective tags, when taken in aggregate, allow patterns to emerge from independent and seemingly random contributions. Wikipedia notes that this feature first began appearing in a variety of social software in 2004.

In days past, as we previously mentioned, the resources for incorporating images into classroom teaching were limited to low-resolution overhead transparencies and slide

TABLE 2. Potential Uses of Digital Images in Core Content Areas

	SCIENCE	LANGUAGE ARTS	MATHEMATICS	SOCIAL STUDIES
CATEGORY	■ data collection ■ scientific visualization ■ presentation of evidence	■ imagery in reading ■ bridge to writing ■ digital storytelling	■ mathematical analysis ■ mathematical transformations ■ problem solving context	■ primary digital sources ■ community connection ■ tool for social inquiry

projection machines. Today, sites such as Flikr can help students and teachers acquire images (many of the images posted are made freely available for educational use through open source licensing) and communicate and share products with an audience that can include parents, the community, and other schools.

Similarly, the recently launched Ourmedia site (**www.ourmedia.org**) was developed through a collaborative, open source approach with the following mission:

THE IDEA IS PRETTY SIMPLE: People who create video, music, photos, audio clips and other personal media can store their stuff for free on Ourmedia's servers forever, as long as they're willing to share their works with a global audience.

Ourmedia's goal is to expose, advance and preserve digital creativity at the grassroots level. The site serves as a central gathering spot where professionals and amateurs come together to share works, offer tips and tutorials, and interact in a combination community space and virtual library that will preserve these works for future generations. We want to enable people anywhere in the world to tap into this rich repository of media and create image albums, movie and music jukeboxes and more.

There is no charge for this storage, which is available to anyone who wishes to use it.

All of these collaborative capabilities—social bookmarking, collaborative imaging sites, shared authoring embedded in wikis and blogs, and many others that are just emerging—offer the opportunity to mix and combine different pieces for knowledge construction. They are being employed in countless ways for business, for entertainment, and for social organization. The challenge for educators is to be aware that many of their students are already using these tools (or will be in future classes), and to identify ways they can be employed effectively and creatively in education.

Reflective Instructional Practice

SINCE THE invention of the printing press more than 500 years ago, the technology for manipulating text has arguably been far more versatile than the technology for manipulating images. The invention of typewriters in the 19th century allowed individual users to produce text documents that approximated the output quality of a printing press. However, there was no easy way to incorporate images in a typewritten document. A teacher producing class materials could incorporate images only by carefully typing around an open box and inserting a hand drawing or photo.

Even the first word processors privileged text over images. In these early systems, the image was not shown on the screen in the same way as the text, and images could not be as easily manipulated. Most high-stakes tests throughout the 20th century required students to respond to textual instructions and manipulate symbols, but rarely provided any visual cues or exhibits. Until very recently, most teaching materials remained a read-only medium. While students are bombarded throughout the day with countless images from TV, newspapers, and magazines, they are rarely asked to produce their own multimedia materials involving images as well as text.

Today, the technology for manipulating images and incorporating them into instruction is rapidly closing this gap. Powerful, inexpensive tools of all kinds are becoming available. Rather than remaining passive consumers of media produced by others, the next generation will be the first to routinely employ image processing tools in their schoolwork. However, teachers need to reflect carefully on how these tools can best be used to address curricular objectives before benefits in learning and student achievement will be realized.

The examples provided in the content area chapters of part 2 will help teachers take the first steps in this reflective instructional practice. They provide a broad array of illustrative uses intended to stimulate thinking about how this new technology can be used to enhance learning in all subjects.

THIS CHAPTER is based on a May 2004 article by Glen L. Bull and Ann Thompson titled "Establishing a Framework for Digital Images in the School Curriculum" and published in *Learning and Leading with Technology* magazine. The authors wish to acknowledge Ann's valuable contribution to their thinking about the acquire-analyze-create-communicate framework.

CHAPTER 2

Barbara Chamberlin

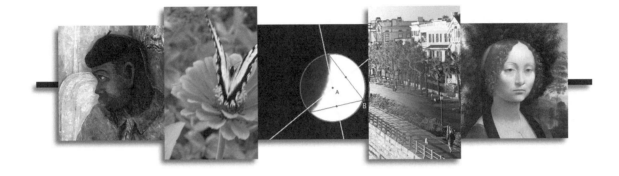

digital photography
for classroom teachers

DIGITAL PHOTOGRAPHY is an appealing technology to use in the classroom because it is rooted in skills that many teachers already have—taking and analyzing photos, and using them to create instructional materials and student projects. Digital photography is different from traditional photography in several ways, however, and understanding those differences will make the process of acquiring, analyzing, creating, and communicating with digital photos much easier. Learning the basic vocabulary and procedures will help teachers choose and use digital cameras and images in ways that support content learning.

Selecting a Digital Camera

AS WITH any major purchase, the first step in selecting a digital camera is to research the options. Several online Web sites such as Digital Photography Review (**www.dpreview.com**) and Digital Camera Resource Page (**www.dcresource.com**) provide excellent reviews of nearly all currently available digital cameras. It is also a good idea to visit a camera store or a large electronics outlet where you can hold and play with as many cameras as possible. By using several, you'll get a feel for which are easy and durable enough to use in the classroom. Look for cameras with menu settings you understand and features familiar to you from traditional cameras, such as auto and manual focus, or the ability to add additional lenses or an external flash.

Digital photography has also introduced new features to cameras. An LCD display on the back of the camera allows the photographer to review photos immediately after taking them—one of the major advantages of digital photography. Unfortunately, these displays take a lot of battery power, so be sure to consider the camera's power supply. Some digital cameras use traditional alkaline batteries that can be expensive to replace and may have a short life span. High-quality rechargeable batteries offer better performance and cheaper operation, but require users to maintain a regular recharging schedule. Spare batteries are a must for cameras that will be used in the field.

Many digital cameras come with a built-in optical zoom lens, enabling close-up and moderate telephoto shots. Some also offer a "digital zoom" option, which involves the internal cropping and magnification of one segment of the image. When using digital zoom, objects will appear larger in the frame, but quality and clarity will be reduced, because the picture will contain fewer pixels (more on pixels in a moment). Consequently, an optical zoom lens is a more usable and important feature.

Chances are your budget will dictate which kind of camera you can purchase. Identify the features that are most important to you and the way you hope to use the camera—zoom, flash, manual controls, macro (close focus) capability, additional lenses, and so on. Then, consider buying the highest megapixel camera in your price range with the features you need.

Megapixels, File Size, and Resolution

DIGITAL IMAGES, whether captured by a digital camera or scanned from a traditional print, are made up of *pixels:* small squares of solid color. When you use software to look very closely at a digital photo, you can actually see the pixels and count them.

One way of measuring a digital photo's size, in fact, is to count the number of pixels in it. When the photo in Figure 1 was taken with a digital camera, it was 2,272 pixels across and 1,704 pixels tall. By multiplying width by height, we know the total number of pixels in that image is 3,871,488.

Photo by Barbara Chamberlin.

FIGURE 1. Digital photos are made of pixels. By zooming in on a digital photo, you can actually see and count the number of solid, square pixels in an image. This photo measures 2,272 wide x 1,704 tall, which equals 3,871,488 pixels.

WHAT IS A MEGAPIXEL?

A *megapixel* is one million pixels. The butterfly image has 3,871,488 pixels in it—approximately 3.9 megapixels.

One measure of camera quality is the total number of pixels it can capture in a single image. A camera that takes 5 megapixel images will generally yield higher quality photos than one that can take only 2 megapixel images.

The more pixels in your image, the smoother and clearer the image will appear (see Figure 2). Of course, the more pixels in your image, the more data your camera and computer have to store for that photo. Just as a letter with 2,000 words in it will require more computer memory than a letter with only 500 words, a digital photo with 3.9 megapixels will take up more space on your hard drive than one with 2 megapixels. The trade-off for higher quality photos, then, is the need for more storage memory, both in the camera and on your computer.

Similarly, many cameras allow you to choose the resolution, or picture size, of the photos you take (up to the camera's maximum number of pixels). You can take photos at lower resolution (fewer pixels) and therefore fit more of them on your camera, or you can change the settings to take fewer photos with more pixels.

Photo by Barbara Chamberlin.

FIGURE 2. More pixels means smoother photos.

The left part of the Figure 2 photo is the smoothest; it has the most pixels in it. As the pixel count decreases left to right, the quality also decreases.

HOW MANY PIXELS DO I NEED?

Photos that will be viewed on a computer screen need only 72 pixels per inch (ppi) to look smooth. However, if you print a photo at 72 ppi, it will look jagged and rough. To look smooth in print, a photo should have at least 150 ppi for printing on a color inkjet printer, or 300 ppi for professional-quality prints.

Before determining the number of pixels you will need, decide how you will generally share and view your photos. If you will mostly be sharing photos on a computer monitor (using e-mail, or Web or presentation software), a 2 megapixel camera will probably be just fine. If you plan to print your images on a regular basis, you may want to consider a camera with a higher megapixel count. Use the chart in Table 1 to help you decide the total number of pixels you need. A 1 megapixel camera will yield photos that look great on screen, even as large as 8 x 10 inches. A 2 megapixel photo will print beautifully at 4 x 6 inches.

In addition to smoother images, additional pixels provide an edge when cropping photos. One of the most common mistakes made by casual photographers is taking a photo from too far away. This can be fixed by cropping the picture and enlarging it. If you have more

TABLE 1. Photo Size and Pixel Size

FINAL SIZE	WEB, E-MAIL, OR PRESENTATION **72 ppi** At 72 pixels per inch…	HOME PRINTING **150 ppi** At 150 pixels per inch…	PROFESSIONAL PRINTING **300 ppi** At 300 pixels per inch…
4 x 6 INCHES	288 x 432 = 124,416 pixels	600 x 900 = 540,000 pixels	1,200 x 1,800 = 2,160,000 pixels (2 megapixels)
5 x 7 INCHES	360 x 504 = 181,440 pixels	750 x 1,050 = 787,500 pixels	1,500 x 2,100 = 3,150,000 pixels (3 megapixels)
8 x 10 INCHES	576 x 720 = 414,720 pixels	1,200 x 1,500 = 1,800,000 pixels (2 megapixels)	2,400 x 3,000 = 7,200,000 pixels (7 megapixels)

pixels to begin with, you can crop out more pixels, and still have enough left to work with (see Figure 3).

Finally, it is important to remember that pixel count is only one determinant of picture quality. The quality of the lens as well as the camera's internal image processing circuitry can greatly affect its output. Some high-quality 2 megapixel cameras can produce images that are just as sharp and color-balanced as cheaper 3 or 4 megapixel models. Be sure to read several reviews of the models you are considering, and don't make your decision based solely on a single specification such as pixel count.

WHAT IS COMPRESSION?

Another factor that determines the quality of a digital image is file compression. File compression is a set of mathematical algorithms that digital cameras use to reduce the file size of stored photos, without actually changing the photo's dimensions. The trade-off for this smaller file size is picture quality—a highly compressed image may look "noisy" or display strange patterns. If you have enough space to store images, shoot your photos at the highest resolution and lowest compression you can (often referred to as "image quality" or "compression" in camera menu settings).

WHAT FORMAT SHOULD I USE?

The most common format for digital photos—and the one you will probably want to use for your classroom—is JPEG. The JPEG format allows a range of compression options, giving you great quality at a large file size and poorer quality at a smaller file size. Most digital cameras shoot JPEGs as the default. JPEGs are easily integrated into Web pages, e-mail, and most software applications. All JPEGs will have *some* compression (thus lowering the quality of your image), but it is unlikely you will notice this difference in classroom or consumer-level uses.

Photos by Barbara Chamberlin.

FIGURE 3. Above is a photo before cropping. This original photo is 2,272 x 1,704 pixels, or 3,871,488. Below is the same photo after cropping. Once the excess pixels are cropped out, the image is 924 x 693 pixels, or only 640,332.

The TIFF format is frequently used for higher-end print materials, such as high-quality posters or brochures. The TIFF format allows you to save your image with compression or without (for highest quality). Many digital cameras also allow you to shoot in one of the "raw" formats. Raw formats are different from the other image formats, as they save very specific information about each pixel in the image, allowing software to parse the image later (instead of parsing and saving the image immediately). Photographers wishing to have very detailed control over their images when editing may choose to use a raw format because of the flexibility it provides. The raw format can be difficult to work with, especially as it is not just one format type, but a family of formats. Your album software may not be able to open them, and you often need to download special software from the manufacturer of the camera. The file sizes can also be quite large.

If your camera is able to store photos in more than one format, you should be able to change this setting in your menu settings. For the greatest ease of use, select JPEG.

Storing and Organizing Photos

HOW DO DIGITAL CAMERAS STORE PHOTOS?

Most digital cameras store photos on some kind of removable card or disk (also called "removable media"). Several types of media are available for cameras—Compact Flash cards, Smart Media cards, even rewritable CDs or DVDs for very large cameras. The kind of media your camera uses really isn't important, but understanding how the media work is.

Removable media come in various sizes. New cameras often come with a small card— 16 MB or 32 MB. The number of pictures this card will hold depends on the image size and file compression you choose, but generally a card of this size will hold only a handful of high-resolution images. Remember, the larger the image size (the more megapixels), the fewer pictures your card will be able to hold. You will probably want to invest in a larger card, or several smaller cards so that each student or photographer has his or her own. Many teachers find it easier for all students to have their own personal memory card rather than trying to keep track of individual student photos on a larger, communal card.

Moving or downloading images from the camera to the computer can usually be done in either of two ways: using a cable to plug the camera directly into the computer, or removing the memory card from the camera and using a card reader attached to the computer. You can delete the images on the camera once they have been copied or leave them on the card in the camera.

HOW SHOULD I STORE AND EDIT PHOTOS FOR THE CLASSROOM?

Most digital cameras ship with image capture and editing software from the manufacturer. Some of these programs have organizational features that allow you to group photos by photographer or topic. At the very least, you'll want to create an organizational

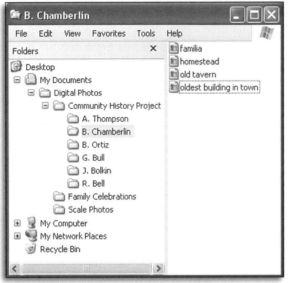

FIGURE 4. Consider placing all your digital photos in one folder on your hard drive, with additional folders for organization.

Screenshot reprinted with permission from Microsoft Corporation.

structure on your hard drive to keep photos organized. Try to store all photos in a central folder, creating subfolders for each student or topic (see Figure 4).

Your camera will typically number photos when saving them to the removable media. As soon as you view photos on your computer, consider renaming them so that you can identify them later. If your computer has the capability to write to a CD-ROM or Zip drive, consider storing photos for each student on individual disks.

To organize your pictures, the best option is to utilize an album program. Sometimes, the software that comes with your camera will include a basic album program that allows you to view thumbnails of photos, organize them by date, assign keywords, and rename them as needed (see Figure 5). More full-featured album programs allow you to create custom layouts for your photos: photo album pages, greeting cards, or multiphoto layouts for printing. Popular album programs (such as those in Adobe Photoshop Elements and Microsoft Digital Image Pro) are available at discounted prices for educators, while Apple's iPhoto software is preinstalled on new Macintosh computers and is also available in Apple's affordable iLife software.

Album programs also allow you to do simple photo editing, such as cropping, removing red eye, making simple color adjustments, and exporting for use in e-mail, Web, or presentation programs. Most of your typical editing needs can be met using an album program. More advanced editing programs offer a number of special features (such as adding text and arrows to a photograph, or applying special effects) and give you much greater control over the final image.

Sharing Photos

HOW DO I PRINT MY PHOTOS?

Low-cost inkjet printers can print photos with surprisingly good results. Especially when printing on photo-quality paper and printed at high resolution (150-300 ppi), inkjet printers can produce crisp and colorful images that will satisfy most classroom needs. Digital photo printers are also available that print directly from some digital cameras. This immediacy is great when students need to share their photos right after taking them. A word of caution, however; while most inkjet printers are affordable to buy, replacement ink cartridges can be quite expensive if you do a lot of printing. Photos printed on inkjet printers are usually not waterproof, and they don't typically hold their color for many years.

If you want higher quality images for long-term storage, consider having your pictures printed professionally. Many photo kiosks at photo labs and discount stores accept memory cards directly from the camera (or images saved to a CD-ROM). Quality and color balance can vary from kiosk to kiosk, as can cost.

Screenshot courtesy of Apple.

FIGURE 5. Most album software allows you to view thumbnails of photos, rename them, assign keywords, and sort them into groups.

Another option, particularly for those with a high-speed connection to the Internet, is online printing. Online printers take your credit card number and mailing address, and allow you to post photos to their servers. Most album programs give you simple access to online printing programs; you select photos in the album to print, enter your credit card number, and the program sends the photos to the print house for you. Prices vary, as do special features, such as printing a photo on a T-shirt or coffee mug. While there is a delay of several days while the print house mails the photos to you, the quality is usually very good and prints are indistinguishable from traditional film prints.

When preparing your photos for print, be sure to size them appropriately. Use an image editing program to resize your image to the desired print size and resolution (see Figure 6).

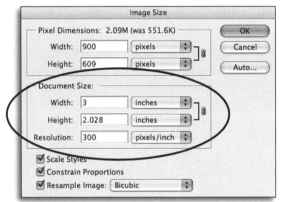

FIGURE 6. Resize images as needed for print. Use the command to resize images in your editing program to size your photo appropriately. For resolution, select 150 ppi for home printing or 300 ppi for professional printing. Then set the image's width or height.

Screenshot reprinted with permission from Adobe Systems Incorporated.

HOW DO I PREPARE PHOTOS FOR E-MAIL, WEB SITES, AND PRESENTATIONS?

One of the most common mistakes that people new to digital photography make is placing images into e-mails or presentations that are too large and memory-intensive. The images may appear too big on the screen or dramatically increase the file size of a Web page or presentation. Particularly when placing photos in a presentation program, be sure to use a photo editing program to size them appropriately (see Figure 7). Remember that any image displayed onscreen (Web, e-mail, or presentation) will look fine at 72 ppi.

Introducing Students to Digital Photography

EVEN WHEN developing picture-taking skills is not the primary reason for introducing digital cameras to students, it is still a good idea to provide students in all grade levels with some general photography instruction before letting them loose in the field or classroom. Students should feel comfortable using a camera and downloading their images from the camera to a computer. Additionally, they should understand some of the features specific to digital photography, such as image editing and manipulation (see chapter 3) and issues related to copyright and fair use (see chapter 4).

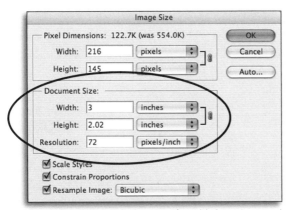

Screenshot reprinted with permission from Adobe Systems Incorporated.

FIGURE 7. Resize images as needed for onscreen. Use the command to resize images in your editing program to size your photo appropriately. For resolution, select 72 ppi for e-mail, Web sites, and presentations. Then set the image's width or height.

WHAT DO STUDENTS NEED TO KNOW ABOUT USING A DIGITAL CAMERA?

General photography instruction helps new photographers become familiar with typical camera controls and shooting options, and become more aware of both what they are photographing and how. It is likely that every group of students will include a few who have some experience taking pictures with different types of cameras and a few who are completely unfamiliar with photography. When you first bring a camera into the classroom, allow students some time to hold it in their hands and familiarize themselves with the various buttons, knobs, and features. Encourage students to follow along as you briefly review the basics of using a digital camera, such as using auto focus and turning off the flash (see Table 2).

It can also be helpful to show pictures of the controls on two different cameras, high-lighting how to do these basics on each (see Figure 8).

HOW IMPORTANT IS PHOTOGRAPHIC SKILL?

Although photographic skill is not likely to be the emphasis of the digital image work in your classroom, helping students to take better photographs may be worth the time and effort. The most common errors amateur photographers make include not taking enough photos, using the focus features on the camera incorrectly, and not getting close enough to the subject. Encourage your students to use the display on the back of the camera to frame their subject before they take the shot. Encourage them to take more pictures than they think they need, knowing they may keep only one for every 10 they delete.

If you do not have time to instruct students on digital image editing basics, give your students resources for learning on their own time, such as Web tutorials. Many digital photography tutorials can be found online (such as those at **www.shortcourses.com**), and students often take up photography as a hobby once they are exposed to it.

TABLE 2. Key Camera Concepts

USING ANY DIGITAL CAMERA
In your instruction, emphasize features available on *all* digital cameras, encouraging learners to follow along on their own camera. Key concepts include: ■ turning the camera on ■ taking photos ■ viewing photos on the camera ■ using the zoom lens ■ using the built-in flash ■ choosing among flash, compression, and image size options ■ using auto focus ■ storing images (the number of images a memory card will hold) and the relationship between storage and compression or quality settings ■ deleting images

PHOTOGRAPHIC SCAVENGER HUNT

Once students have learned the basics of using the camera and have some idea about how to take better photos, give them an opportunity to practice immediately. A photographic scavenger hunt provides an excellent way for learners to become comfortable with the camera while reviewing the basic competencies. Prepare a checklist for photographers and give them 20 minutes to take the required photographs. The example scavenger hunt in Table 3 can easily be adapted for inside or outside settings.

FIGURE 8. Use photos to demonstrate similar steps on different cameras. You can't possibly provide instruction on every type of digital camera your learners may have. Use photos to highlight features on two different kinds of cameras, and encourage learners to explore with you on their own camera.

Reward your students by giving them tangible evidence of their skill. Make sure your learners receive a copy of one of their best prints. If you have time, consider having their favorite image enlarged, matted, and framed in an inexpensive frame, and allow them to sign and name their print. Enabling them to share their work in this way will help students feel more professional and interested in improving their skills (Figure 9).

Conclusion

FORTUNATELY, DIGITAL photography can have a powerful effect on learning in the classroom regardless of the technical expertise of the teacher, the quality of the images that students take, or the settings used on the camera. It is easy to feel overwhelmed by new technologies and terminologies. Just remember that it is more important to think carefully about how you want to use digital images to enhance teaching and learning (the subject of the content area chapters in part 2) than it is to understand all the settings on a camera menu.

TABLE 3. Familiarizing Students with Camera Use

SAMPLE PHOTOGRAPHIC SCAVENGER HUNT
(Appropriate for all grade levels)

Take your camera outside for 20 minutes and shoot each of the following:

- **Cat Cam:** Imagine a cat has the camera. What would it take a photo of?
  (Purpose: changing camera position)

- **Who's Got the Blues?:** Take a photo of something that has a lot of blue tones (but not just the sky).
  (Purpose: looking at colors)

- **Hugantic Ant:** Take a photo that makes something small seem really big.
  (Purpose: experimenting with perspective, depth of field, and close-up focus)

- **Shaq Cam:** Take a photo with the camera held as high as you can reach.
  (Purpose: changing camera position, using auto focus)

- **A Motion Picture:** Take a photo of a fast-moving object, keeping the camera's viewfinder framed on the object as it moves by.
  (Purpose: learning camera panning)

- **Lean Scene:** Tilt the camera and take a photo.
  (Purpose: experimenting with camera position/orientation)

- **Look on the Bright Side:** Take a photo of another person's head and shoulders, using the flash outside, with the subject standing in shadow.
  (Purpose: using fill flash/back lighting)

- **Assimilate This:** Take a photo of at least three of the same things in a row. Focus on the one that is closest to you.
  (Purpose: experimenting with patterns, depth of field, and auto focus)

This scavenger hunt was developed by Darrel Pehr and is used with permission.

Photo by Pamela Martinez.

FIGURE 9. Encourage ownership by giving learners prints of their favorite photo. Consider enlarging a student's favorite photo and placing it in an inexpensive matted frame so the student can hang it on a wall at home.

A great deal can be learned about the technical aspects of digital photography simply through experience and experimentation. Ultimately, photography helps us *see* better—an important step in learning from the world around us.

CHAPTER 3

*Tom Hammond and
Richard Sebastian*

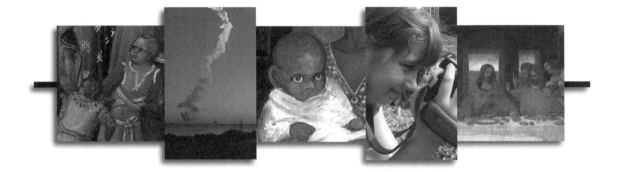

digital image and video editing software

THE INSTRUCTIONAL activities described in this book all involve the use of digital images or video, whether captured by digital cameras, scanned from prints, or downloaded from the Web. In many cases, these images will require some kind of editing or manipulation—cropping and resizing, changing contrast and color balance, fixing red eye and other common image flaws, or even adding layers and other elements to the picture. Digital video may require editing such as reorganizing scenes, cutting frames, or adding audio tracks. This chapter introduces you to software resources available for digital image and video editing. We describe common features of these programs and suggest which ones are most suited for use in the classroom.

Working with Images

NUMEROUS IMAGE editing packages are available. In fact, it is very likely that your digital camera or scanner was bundled together with the manufacturer's own image editing software. Both Microsoft Windows and the Mac OS include basic image editors, and some office suites (such as Microsoft Office) include photo editing software. In addition, several free programs are available for download on the Internet, such as the GIMP (Gnu Image Manipulation Program) and Picasa, or you can purchase more advanced packages such as Macromedia Fireworks, Microsoft Digital Image Pro, Adobe Photoshop Elements, Ulead PhotoImpact, or Jasc Paint Shop Pro.

With so many options to choose from, it can be overwhelming for those new to digital photography to determine which program best suits their needs. The purpose of this chapter is to introduce the most popular choices, using them to illustrate editing processes and features you may want to employ in the classroom. We have separated these editors into "basic" and "advanced" categories. The basic editors are easy to use but contain relatively few features. The advanced editors are more powerful but often have a steeper learning curve.

BASIC IMAGE EDITORS

Microsoft Paint and iPhoto—which come preinstalled on Windows and Macintosh computers, respectively—are examples of basic image editors. While the editors vary widely in appearance (see Figures 1 and 2), they do have certain features in common.

Screenshot courtesy of Apple.

FIGURE 1. An image displayed in iPhoto.

FIGURE 2. An image displayed in MS Paint.

First, all image editors allow you to rotate or resize an image. Most also allow you to select some or all of the image, copy or cut your selection, and then paste it into another document or program. Typically, the software offers basic controls for cropping an image (i.e., selecting part of it and discarding the rest).

Almost all basic image editors also allow you to draw or write on the image. Just as with a word processor, you can choose the font, font size, color, and text effects; you can also select the color and size of the lines you draw. Be sure to select colors and sizes that stand out on your image, or add a background that will allow the text to be read easily (compare the lettering in Figures 2 and 3).

Some image editors, particularly ones that come with a digital camera or scanner, also have special features to improve photo quality, such as removing red eye or enhancing the color balance.

Two important photo editing tools all students should know about are Undo and Save As. These are important when working in any application, but especially when working with graphic images. Children need to feel free to experiment when modifying images, and knowing that they can undo a line or save a version of a file under a different name will allow them to tinker with an image without worrying about ruining the original picture.

FIGURE 3. An image displayed in the GIMP. Note the Undo History (lower left) and Layers (lower right) features.

ADVANCED IMAGE EDITORS

Advanced image editors include Adobe Photoshop Elements, Microsoft Digital Image Pro, Ulead PhotoImpact, and the GIMP. The latter can be downloaded for free, but most advanced editing programs must be purchased. Discounts for educators are common.

These editors are extremely powerful. Almost any modification or special effect that the user can imagine can be implemented using these advanced programs. However, the software can be challenging to use. In addition to the usual buttons and pull-down menus, these advanced editors have "panels" or "dialog boxes" that can be called up to control more complex tools (see Figure 3). For example, the GIMP editor includes a common feature called Undo History that acts as an advanced version of Undo, allowing users to undo every change they have made to the image, step by step. While this Undo History feature is a powerful tool, it can be difficult for students to locate and confusing for them to use.

Two other important features are Layers and Tools. Layers work much like overhead transparencies. In Figure 3, the text ("Filming a spider web") is actually on a layer superimposed on top of the base image. This allows users to make changes to the text layer, such as rotating it or adding a drop-shadow, without altering the background layer.

Layers can be linked, merged, rearranged, and made invisible or semitransparent. Often you might want to select a piece of the image, cut it, and move it to a new layer. Advanced image editors offer many options for selection tools, from the simple (such as rectangular or oval regions) to the complex (selecting color regions or using the freehand lasso) to the magical (using tools such as Magic Wand or Intelligent Scissors). Once a region is selected, you can move it, recolor it, resize it, stretch it, make it semitransparent, or transplant it to another image.

In addition to these two features, advanced image editors offer many other utilities, such as filters, cloning and pattern stamps, smudgers, dodge, burn, and more. Encourage students who have learned the basics to experiment with these more advanced selections; you will likely be surprised by the professional-looking results.

File types become especially important when using advanced editors. Most of these editors have their own "native" file type. For example, Adobe image files save as PSD (see Figure 4) and GIMP files save as XCF. These specialized file types save the complex formatting information that goes into the layers, alpha channels, and other advanced features. However, these specialized file types are frequently incompatible with other programs. If you want to insert an Adobe file into a presentation, you will first have to select Save As or Save a Copy and create a version of the image in a more common file type, such as JPEG.

Screenshot reprinted with permission from Adobe Systems Incorporated.

FIGURE 4. An image displayed in Adobe Photoshop Elements. Note the different file types that can be produced.

INSERTING IMAGES INTO DOCUMENTS OR PRESENTATIONS

After capturing and editing an image, you may wish to insert it into a document or presentation. In most cases, this is a simple process of selecting Insert from within your word processing or presentation program and then selecting the image file from its saved location. Once the image has been inserted into a document, you can usually continue to make changes to it. Microsoft Word and Microsoft PowerPoint allow the user to crop or rotate images, adjust brightness or contrast, or change images from color to black and white or watermark. However, it is generally a much better idea to do all the editing with an image editor *before* inserting into the document.

RECOMMENDATIONS

For very basic tasks, MS Paint or iPhoto (or Kid Pix for younger ages) are good choices for classroom use. Students may already be familiar with these tools from previous experience at school or at home. For those new to these programs, they are fairly easy to learn, and the tools remain visible all the time.

For more advanced tasks, Adobe Photoshop Elements is very powerful yet affordable and has an interface that is reasonably easy to use. The tabs for the various dialogs are always visible and can be pulled out into separate windows. Photoshop Elements is also supported by many training and help resources for both teachers and students. Several books are available that demonstrate all the program's features, and the software comes with built-in tutorial files that illustrate key concepts. Photographer Jay Arraich also has an interest in Photoshop and Photoshop Elements and maintains free how-to materials on his Web site, **www.arraich.com**.

Macromedia Fireworks is another advanced editor that bears mention. Fireworks is similar to Photoshop Elements in that it uses layers, has advanced selection tools, tracks an image's "history" as changes are made, and saves images in its own native file format. However, Fireworks is one program in a suite of software tools for creating Web sites, and thus has many features that facilitate using images in Web design, such as animation, frames, and image libraries. If you are already familiar with Macromedia's other products (such as Dreamweaver or Flash), Fireworks is easy to learn because it uses the same organizational layout and has similar tools and features. Beginners will probably find Fireworks' multiple panels dauntingly complex (see Figure 5). However, the program works pretty much the same way as Photoshop Elements, and once your students are familiar with its layout, it provides a great introduction to Macromedia's other useful tools.

A final advanced editor to consider is the GIMP, which can be downloaded for free at **http://gimp.org**. The GIMP is as versatile as Photoshop, but the navigation is Linux-style and is therefore very different from most Mac or Windows programs. However, one appealing feature of the GIMP is that it can read other programs' native formats, such as PSD (Photoshop Elements) and PNG (Macromedia Fireworks).

Fireworks product © 2005 Macromedia, Inc.

FIGURE 5. An image displayed in Macromedia Fireworks. Note the image library at right, allowing multiple copies of the spider graphic to be pulled onto the main image.

The other advanced editors from Microsoft, Ulead, and Jasc offer many of the same features as those described, with different price tags and varying degrees of user-friendliness. If you or your school already has one of these programs, take some time to experiment to determine whether it is accessible enough for students at your grade level.

Video Editing

YOU CAN import and edit video captured with a digital camcorder using nonlinear video editing software. This software can also be used to incorporate your completed digital still images into a video. In the following paragraphs we describe the general hardware and software specifications of typical consumer-level nonlinear video editors.

CAPTURING FOOTAGE

First of all, if you want to use video footage captured with a digital camcorder, you will need to find a way to get your footage from the DV tape in the camcorder to your computer's hard drive. If your computer is equipped with a FireWire card (also called an IEEE 1394 card), using a FireWire cable is the fastest and most effective way to transfer video

Photo by Lynn Bell.

FIGURE 6. A FireWire (IEEE 1394) port on a computer.

(Figure 6). FireWire cards are fairly inexpensive and easy to install. If FireWire is not an option, you can also use a slower USB connection.

Once your camera is connected to your computer, you can transfer the video footage to your computer's hard drive.

A newer generation of tapeless digital video cameras is emerging that saves video directly to a "microdrive," a miniature hard disk that is also used in some digital still cameras and portable music devices. These devices can be removed to allow the data to be uploaded to the computer using a memory card reader.

It is also possible to capture footage from VHS tapes using an additional piece of hardware, often called a "breakout box," attached to your computer. This box allows your computer to convert the VHS tape's analog signal into a digital one. One of the nonlinear video editors reviewed below, Pinnacle Studio 9, offers a pricier version of Studio 9 that includes a breakout box for this type of conversion.

STORING VIDEO FILES

Another important consideration when working with digital video is the amount of hard-drive space you will need for your project. Digital video files eat up huge amounts of memory: four minutes of high-quality video can occupy as much as 1 gigabyte (GB) of memory on your hard drive! It is essential to have a hard drive with at least 20 GB of available space (and preferably much more) before you begin working with digital video footage of any length. If your internal hard drive is too small or too full, consider purchasing a removable, external hard drive to store your captured video and video projects. External hard drives come in sizes from 40 GB to 500 GB or more.

In addition to video storage requirements, there are other technical considerations to keep in mind when working with video. Because of the memory demands they make on your computer, most video editing programs have minimum technical requirements that your computer must meet in order to handle video playback. These specifications include the speed of your computer's processor, the speed of its graphic card, the type of audio card, and the amount of RAM. These requirements are typically listed on the box that accompanies the software. Most newer computers are equipped to meet the requirements of the video editing programs profiled in this chapter. If you are in doubt or have an older computer running Windows, you can go to the Windows Control Panel, click on the System icon, and check to see whether your computer meets the software specifications. For a Mac running OS X, click the System Profiler in the Utilities folder.

Video Editing Software

BECAUSE OF the popularity of digital video, a wide selection of video editors are currently on the market. These range from basic programs provided free with new computers to professional-grade software that can cost thousands of dollars. Regardless of the one you choose, some basic features are common to all.

NONLINEAR EDITING

While traditional movies are made up of long reels of processed film that have been physically cut and spliced together, digital videos are processed and edited electronically on a computer. Consequently, digital video can be edited applying the same techniques used to edit a text document on a computer. For example, the order in which the footage was originally shot doesn't matter; nonlinear editors let you copy, cut, and paste video like you would text. You can also easily make digital duplicates of captured video footage. Perhaps most important, if you do make a mistake while editing, you can simply undo the last action with a quick keystroke.

Almost all video editors allow you to divide your captured video file into a manageable set of *clips*, allowing you to organize scenes easily, pick out your best takes, assemble action/reaction shots, trim down overlong shots, and delete entire segments.

TRANSITIONS

Transitions are placed *between* video clips to affect how the clips flow together in your movie. For example, you can add a popular transition called a *dissolve* so that one clip fades in as the previous one fades out, allowing the two to overlap briefly. Another transition, called a *wipe*, quickly wipes one image away like a windshield wiper and replaces it with the first image of the next clip. Rather than having your images and clips play one after another, transitions let your clips interact, which can enhance the video's rhythm, pacing, and overall style.

EFFECTS

While transitions are inserted *between* clips, effects are added *to* the actual video clip. For example, adding a pan-and-scan effect to a still image in your video lets you zoom in on an object in the image, such as a person's face; or you can add a sepia effect that makes a video clip look washed out and tinted, like an old movie. Effects can change a movie clip's basic attributes, such as brightness, contrast, color, speed, and direction (forward and reverse), as well as make more elaborate changes, such as the expensive digital effects found in science fiction movies. Effects can be fun to play with, and when used effectively, they help to enhance the story you are telling with your video.

TITLES

You can easily add text to your video using titles. You can insert the title of your video at the beginning of the movie, and add credits at the end. You can also use titles within your video to show important dates, names, settings and locations, and quotes.

Titles can be added to your movie in two different ways: as separate clips with colored backgrounds, or as overlays that appear on top of the video image, like a subtitle. Most software programs allow you to choose the font, size, style, duration, and color of your titles.

AUDIO EDITING

Most basic nonlinear video editors allow you to add additional audio tracks to the sound captured with your video, such as narration, sound effects, and music. Most of the basic programs allow only for rudimentary audio editing, however, and have a limited number

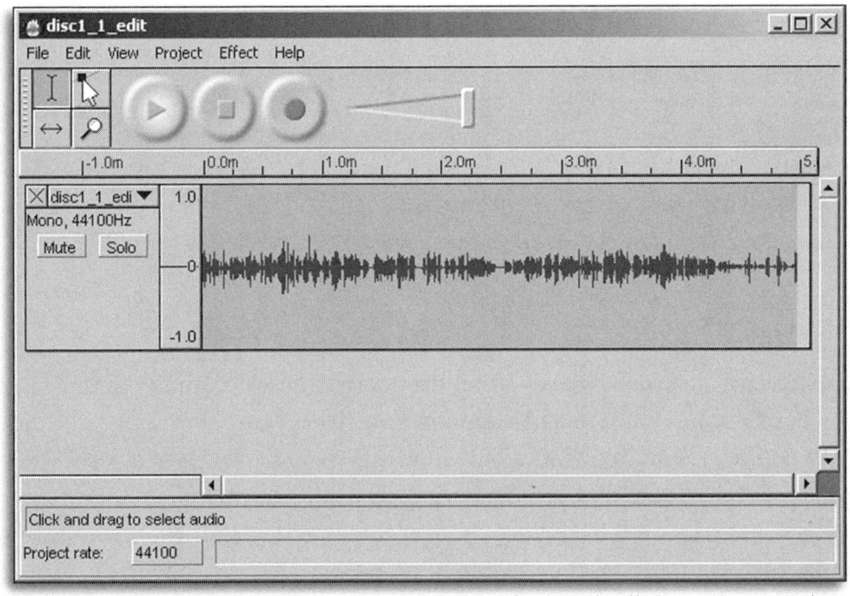

Screenshot of product authored by Dominic Mazzoni, © Audacity.

FIGURE 7. The Audacity interface for editing sound files.

of available audio tracks. Like video, audio can be divided into clips that can be cut, copied, and pasted, allowing you to delete any mistakes and use only the best parts. It is also very easy to adjust a clip's volume level to make the audio fade in and out.

Another option is to work on the sound clips with a separate audio editor such as Audacity, which is a free program available for download at **http://audacity.sourceforge. net** (see Figure 7). Finished audio clips can then be imported into your video project. Almost all video editors accept audio files saved in the WAV and MP3 formats.

RENDERING

Until your movie is *rendered*, it resides on your computer simply as an indexed collection of video and audio clips, still images, transitions, effects, titles, and so on; all of these separate files are scattered here and there on your hard drive. Rendering your video takes this collection of files and assembles them into a single standalone file that can be played on a computer. Video editors often render videos in their own unique file formats, which may limit where you can play the completed video. For example, to play a video saved as a MOV file (the file format for Apple's QuickTime), your computer must have the QuickTime Player. Similarly, videos saved as WMV files can be played only on computers that have Windows Media Player installed. The good news is that most video players are dual platform—that is, they work on both PCs and Macs—and can be downloaded from the Internet for free.

Still, the more rendering options you have, the better. More powerful video editors let you convert your video to a VCD (video CD) or DVD.

WORKING WITH STILL IMAGES IN A VIDEO EDITOR

Video editors do not limit you to using only video. Most video editors allow you to import digital still images to use with your full-motion video clips. You can also create a video composed entirely of still images, a popular technique used in digital storytelling and documentary films, or with a collection of time-lapse images. Creating a video using only still images is an especially useful technique for classrooms with technical limitations. Digital images use far less hard-drive space and require less memory from your computers.

The most recent version of Elements, Photoshop Elements 3 (available for Windows only), provides a quick and easy way to create a slideshow from still images. Besides its powerful image editing features, Photoshop Elements 3 also allows you to drag digital images from your hard drive onto the Element's storyboard. From there, you can rearrange the order and duration of each slide, include transitions between slides, add narration and music, and insert titles and credits, producing a movie file that can be played on a computer or on a television as a video CD. Keep in mind that Elements allows you to import digital images only. You cannot import digital video.

You can also create a "video" with still images using common presentation software, such as Microsoft PowerPoint. Like Photoshop Elements, PowerPoint allows you to create an automated slideshow from digital images, to which you can add audio such as music or narration. Although cost effective and easy to do, PowerPoint effects (called *animations*) tend to be limited, and the end result can be a bit choppy and uneven.

Recommended Video Editors for the Classroom

FOR WINDOWS COMPUTERS

A variety of video editing programs are available for Windows computers. We recommend the following for classrooms.

Windows Movie Maker. Movie Maker comes free with the Windows XP operating system, which makes it an easy (if limited) choice for use in the classroom. Like Apple's iMovie, Movie Maker is easy to learn and has a simple, user-friendly interface (see Figure 8). Although it was designed as a video editor, it seems to perform best when working with still images.

Screenshot reprinted with permission from Microsoft Corporation.

FIGURE 8. The Microsoft Movie Maker interface with several movie clips on the timeline.

Pinnacle Studio. If funds are available, a good choice for a PC-based video editor is Pinnacle Studio. Pinnacle Studio 9 is the latest version. While the program costs around $100, it handles video more flexibly than Movie Maker. It also has many more features than Movie Maker; for example, it offers dual audio tracks compared to Movie Maker's single audio track. Pinnacle Studio also allows you to render your final video into a variety of file formats, including DVD. It has an easy-to-use interface that can be learned quickly (see Figure 9).

FIGURE 9. The Pinnacle Studio editing interface, including the preview window, timeline, and a selection of clips.

Ulead Video Studio. Another good choice for PCs is Ulead's Video Studio. This video editing software offers similar features found in the other editors already mentioned, such as capturing digital video; editing clips; applying titles, transitions, and effects; and creating VCDs or DVDs. One of Ulead's greatest strengths is its simple and easy-to-use interface, which takes users through a seven-step video creation process. Other notable features of Ulead are its ability to produce slideshows from digital still images, a versatile set of DVD creation tools, and a good selection of video effects.

FOR MACINTOSH COMPUTERS

Excellent video editing programs are also available for Macintosh computers. Here are our classroom recommendations.

iMovie. For Mac users, iMovie is probably the best choice for making videos. iMovie is included in the Mac operating system, and besides being free, iMovie produces high-quality, professional-looking videos. It can be learned fairly quickly and offers a good selection of editing tools and a user-friendly interface.

Final Cut Express. Another option for the Mac user is the Mac-only Final Cut Express. Final Cut Express is a pared down version of Final Cut Pro, a more complex, professional-grade video editor. Final Cut Express costs approximately $150 and should be chosen only by teachers in need of a more comprehensive set of editing tools for their videos. Unlike iMovie, Final Cut Express takes time to learn and can be intimidating for the novice user.

Photo Story Editors

A NEW class of software has recently emerged called "photo story editors." These are special-purpose tools that allow users to combine pictures with narrative to create a story. Microsoft recently released Photo Story 3, which is available as a free download at **www.microsoft.com/windowsxp/using/digitalphotography/photostory/default.mspx**.

With Photo Story 3, users are taken step by step through the process of creating a digital story, from selecting the images they want to use, to adding titles, effects, narration, and music. The software then saves the finished story in a file format playable on any computer with Windows Media Player installed. While Photo Story also offers some basic image editing capabilities, its main function is producing digital stories.

Conclusion

THIS CHAPTER has given you some starting points for choosing and using digital image and video editing software. Although these software tools will undoubtedly evolve in the years to come, the features most appropriate for classroom use (such as ease of use and low cost) will likely remain the same. Remember, too, that educational versions of these commercial products are generally available to teachers at lower cost.

CHAPTER 4

Elizabeth Langran

digital images
and **copyright**

IT'S EASY to imagine the following scenarios: a teacher constructs a Web page for a social studies class using historical images downloaded from the National Archives Web site. Meanwhile, a student grabs an image from Google, uses Adobe Photoshop to manipulate it, drops it into an iMovie video clip, adds an MP3 of a popular song as a soundtrack, and creates a digital story. You may not even have to imagine these things—something similar may already be happening on a regular basis in your school. In this age of peer-to-peer file swapping and cut and paste from the Web, anything goes, right?

Well, perhaps not. These "original" works are being constructed using sounds and images created by other artists.

The idea of original "authorship" is becoming increasingly attenuated and confusing. While free and ubiquitous programs such as Movie Maker and iMovie make it easy for students to become active creators of digital media (not just passive observers), the potential for misuse of copyrighted material represents a tremendous challenge for schools and teachers. Learning to navigate the murky and ever-changing current of copyright law has never been more difficult.

A work need not have a copyright symbol anywhere on it to be protected by copyright law. Any work created in any tangible form of expression—printed text, a photo or film, a piece of music, a Web page—is automatically copyrighted, and remains protected for many years after the creator's death. New technologies, of course, have created new gray areas and unforeseen circumstances that will require ongoing legal interpretation. Copyright law is not a fixed entity; instead, it is malleable and constantly changing in response to the influence of interested parties. In recent years, technology has been the catalyst for major revisions of copyright law, as legislators try to find a balance between corporate interests and consumer rights.

It is understandable that many educators are confused by the changes in copyright legislation. While it is important that teachers learn how to properly respect the rights of copyright holders in their classroom, it is equally important that they know how to take advantage of the tremendous opportunities for learning offered by new media technologies. This chapter will give you a good start in that direction.

Fair Use in the Classroom

TEACHERS AND students can legally use copyrighted material without the author's permission if it falls under "fair use" guidelines. Section 107 of the 1976 Copyright Act addresses the question of fair use; this section reads (in part): "The fair use of a copyrighted work, including such use by reproduction ... for purposes such as criticism, comment, news reporting, teaching, ... scholarship, or research, is not an infringement of copyright."

In order to qualify for fair use, four factors must be weighed:

1. *Purpose of Use.* The work must be used for legitimate scholarship and/or nonprofit, educational purposes.

2. *Nature of the Work.* Creative works are afforded greater copyright protection than factual works.

3. *Amount Used.* Only a small percentage of the entire work may be copied for educational uses.

4. *Effect on the Market.* Potential commercial sales must not be affected.

To use copyrighted material without permission, students and teachers must employ this four-factor test. For example, if a student wants to copy a cartoon character from the Web for use in a multimedia presentation, each factor must be considered separately to determine whether fair use applies. In this case, the purpose for the use (scholarly) and its effect on the market (none) would probably outweigh the nature of the work (creative) and the amount being used (using an image is generally considered using the whole work). As long as the project is shown only in the classroom or at home, this would probably be interpreted as fair use even though only two of the factors are strongly in favor.

Some teachers may be familiar with the rule that no more than five images by any one artist and no more than 10% from a published collective work may be used. This rule was suggested several years ago by special interest groups in a document titled "Classroom Guidelines" (see **www.publishers.org/about/copyqa.cfm**). Although these guidelines were never enacted by the federal government as part of the fair use statute and thus are not law, many school districts have adopted these guidelines. In 1994, the Conference on Fair Use (CONFU) attempted to update the "Classroom Guidelines" to reflect the use of electronic materials, but after many years of deliberations, the CONFU delegates failed to achieve consensus for fair use of electronic media in education.

Easier than trying to negotiate the vagaries of four-factor tests and the "Classroom Guidelines" is using resources that have special permissions already granted for classroom use, such as Creative Commons.

Creative Commons as a Classroom Resource

MUCH OF the evolution of copyright law, both with respect to the crafting of legislation and the subsequent interpretation of it in the courts, has been shaped by corporate stakeholders. Individual consumers typically lack the time or resources to provide input into the process. Both perspectives are important, but the debate is frequently polarized, reflecting either a world of total control of media and materials with all rights reserved, or the anarchy of peer-sharing networks with no safeguards for copyrighted materials.

Creative Commons was established by Lawrence Lessig to offer a middle ground. It involves a vision of copyright licenses in which some rights are reserved, but not all (see **http://creativecommons.org**). Creative Commons recognizes and protects the rights of creators while simultaneously allowing certain educational uses of copyrighted material:

THE FRAMERS of the U.S. Constitution understood that copyright was about balance—a trade-off between public and private gain, society-wide innovation and creative reward ... We want to help restore that sense of balance ... A single goal unites Creative Commons' current and future projects: to build a layer of reasonable, flexible copyright in the face of increasingly restrictive default rules. (**http://creativecommons.org/projects/founderscopyright/**)

For example, the Open Photo site (**http://openphoto.net**) provides images offered under a Creative Commons *Attribution license*, which states that the photographs may be used by others provided that proper attribution is provided. The Creative Commons search engine is a useful tool that facilitates the educational use of Web content. The Creative Commons search engine helps identify materials—images, music, and text—whose authors permit reuse for noncommercial purposes.

Works in the Public Domain

WORKS WHOSE copyright protections have expired enter into the public domain and are available for public use. Most of the images available on the U.S. National Archives Web site (**www.archives.gov**) have entered into the public domain and thus can be used without permission. The teacher in the example at the beginning of this chapter who wants to include National Archive images in her social studies Web site would be free to do so, so long as the images used are in the public domain.

> ### EDUCATIONAL IMAGES
>
> A list of additional Web sites offering images in the public domain or with stated educational use policies may be found in appendix A.

When does copyright protection end and a work enter the public domain? The answer, unfortunately, is an unequivocal "it depends." The term for copyright protection has increased steadily over the years. In 1790, the term of copyright was established as 14 years with the option of a one-time renewal. Subsequent legislation, most recently the Sonny Bono Copyright Term Extension Act (1998), has extended this to the life of the author plus 70 years. The Cornell Copyright Center provides a useful chart that outlines the current copyright terms for various types of work (see **www.copyright.cornell.edu/training/Hirtle_Public_Domain.htm**).

In the digital age, much of the material that falls in the public domain has been accumulated in online centers such as the Library of Congress American Memories Collection (**http://memory.loc.gov/ammem**) and the Electronic Text Center at the University of Virginia (**http://etext.lib.virginia.edu**). These sites make works in the public domain available for convenient searching and downloading.

Meanwhile, the Art Museum Image Consortium or AMICO (**www.amico.org**) offers convenient access to images that are still protected by copyright. The goal of this consortium of art museums is to make a common pool of images available to schools for educational use through a common license. When a school subscribes to AMICO, all the images contributed by its members can be secured.

The easiest way for students to use images without worrying about copyright issues is to use materials they have created themselves. Students are the copyright holders for their own photographs and drawings, a fact teachers should remember before posting student pictures on their own class Web site.

Permission and Attribution

TEACHERS NEED to guide students in exercising good digital citizenship and appropriate behavior. Responsible use of technology should be modeled and discussed with students. *Attribution* and *permission* are two important pieces of responsible use that should be a part of the repertoire of every teacher.

The Web has prompted an unprecedented deluge of self-published materials. Often the individuals who publish such sites are willing to grant permission for educational use. Proper attribution of others' work should always be made, whether the material is copyrighted or in the public domain. Often, students are not aware that attribution for materials copied from Web sites is required.

If you would like to use an image that is protected by copyright and does not fall under fair use, contact the author, artist, photographer, or editor of the image or Web page. You can often find this information at the top or bottom of a Web page under "Contact us" or "About us."

When contacting the copyright holder, be specific about which image you want to use and where you found it, and communicate what you plan to do with the image and whether it will be used for commercial purposes. Include your contact information, and be sure to keep a copy of the permission letter or e-mail you receive in case there are any problems or questions down the road.

When using an image created by someone else, it is always appropriate to give proper attribution to the creator. On the Web, of course, it is not always evident who created an image. If there is no

SEARCHING FOR AN IMAGE ON THE INTERNET

Many of the popular search engines (Google, Alta Vista, Yahoo!) have a tab or drop-down menu to specify that a search is specifically for images. A search engine primarily for digital images is Ditto (**http://ditto.com**). Image searches will typically display the results of your search in thumbnails (smaller versions of the original). Click on the image you want to copy, and you will be taken to the Web site where the image originated. **Caution:** These search engines do not filter out inappropriate visual content. A safer method is to use a directory of images compiled for student use, such as Pics4Learning, found at **http://pics. tech4learning.com**.

indication who is responsible for the image, students should at least indicate the Web site address where the image originated.

At a time when studies indicate that students more often use the Web than a physical library for research and study, it is more important than ever that educators understand copyright and present this information to students in a meaningful context. Although the paradoxes of the current era present teachers with a number of challenges, with a little effort we can find a middle ground between respecting the rights of copyright holders and taking advantage of the learning opportunities presented by new media.

COPYING AN IMAGE FROM A WEB SITE

For PC users, right-click on the image, and choose **Save Image As** or **Save Picture As**, depending on your browser. You will then be prompted to choose a destination on your computer for saving the GIF image or JPEG image. You may want to rename it so that you will remember it more easily, and put it in a place where you can find it again.

This information is not to be considered legal advice. When in doubt about use of a copyrighted work, consult with your institution's legal counsel.

Resources for More Information

PRINT

Carter, T. B., Franklin, M. A., & Wright, J. B. (2003). *The First Amendment and the Fifth Estate* (6th ed.). New York: Foundation Press.

Lessig, L. (2001). *The future of ideas: The fate of the commons in a connected world.* New York: Random House.

Lindsey, M. (2003). *Copyright law on campus.* Pullman, WA: Washington State University Press.

ONLINE

Stanford University Libraries: Copyright and Fair Use: **http://fairuse.stanford.edu**

University of Texas: Fair Use of Copyrighted Materials: **www.utsystem.edu/ogc/intellectualproperty/copypol2.htm**

CHAPTER 5

Julie Springer

every picture
tells a **story**

A PICTURE is worth a thousand words—this saying has become a cliché for a reason. Some of history's most creative individuals, in fields ranging from science to art, have favored visual modes of analysis and thought (West, 1997, p. 11). Yet many school systems still privilege verbal and mathematical skills despite decades of research demonstrating that individuals learn in different ways and that learning is optimized when multiple intelligences are engaged in combination (Gardner, 1985).

The advent of the Web has dramatically changed the type and range of images available in schools, making possible new ways of teaching that incorporate and develop visual intelligence. This chapter explores some of these new opportunities, and in particular the potential for using works of art to promote visual literacy.

The National Gallery of Art has long provided leadership in object-based teaching, working with educators to develop compelling classroom projects that build essential academic and life skills. Selected examples and digital resources from the Gallery's collections are provided in the final section of the chapter.

Why Images in Education? Why Now?

IMAGES ABOUND in our multimedia age. Young people today learn much of what they know through electronic imagery. According to the National Standards for Art Education (Consortium of National Arts Education Associations, 1994), students not only need to learn to communicate verbally, but also need to be able to read and process information visually. Few schools, however, have curricula for developing visual literacy skills (White, 1987).

Happily, we may be on the cusp of significant change. Images may soon become more important in the curriculum as affordable visual computer technologies replace those that are text-based (Bull, Bull, Thomas, & Jordan, 2000; West, 1997). Brain research suggests that images are central to information processing, and work in the field of artificial intelligence is shedding new light on how visual imagery influences memory, thinking, and behavior. As Mary Alice White (1987, p. 44) has argued, "If it is true that our theories of human memory are deeply influenced by advances in computer technology, it is possible that, as the technology moves from being print oriented to being image oriented, our theories of human memory will also become much more image oriented."

Of course, even before the advent of computers, images were critical to conveying information. Graphic images, for example, have always been used to communicate spatial relationships and patterns in ways that words cannot. Information of this kind is often best comprehended holistically and nonsequentially, and visual models support this mode of thinking.

Images and words have always been interdependent. From medieval manuscripts to contemporary preschool storybooks, image and text feed and inform one another. The picture makes the idea tangible; through visualization, the abstract becomes concrete. In much the same way, pictures partner with the spoken word. Verbal analysis is an invaluable aid to understanding what the eye beholds. Discussion and debate build competence in language, critical thinking, and interpersonal skills as students listen to one another and share ideas.

Pictures—whether they exist in the external world or in the mind's eye—play a part in memory and imagination. We dream in pictures, and mental imagery can be a catalyst for the accomplishment of real-life goals. Using visualization techniques, we can improve our performance in sports or other activities, not only persuading ourselves of our potential but also rehearsing the very steps and skills needed to ensure it. Many who practice visualization claim that as much, if not more, can be accomplished through mental imagery as through actual, physical rehearsal.

Although we may intuitively use and respond to an abundance of visual information in daily life, not everyone is adept at interpreting what they see. Visual literacy requires the development of sophisticated viewing skills. The art historian Barbara Stafford (1996, p. 40) maintains, "Educated seeing is precisely about recognizing that information cannot be separated from the manner or style of its display." Artist Ben Shahn (1957, p. 53) states this same idea, only more emphatically: "Form is the very shape of content."

To better understand how an artist's handling of design elements conveys meaning, compare the two narrative images depicting the Old Testament heroine Judith of Bethulia (Figures 1 and 2), shown with the severed head of the Israelites' enemy, the Assyrian general Holofernes.

FIGURE 1. Andrea Mantegna or Follower (possibly Giulio Campagnola), *Judith with the Head of Holofernes,* c. 1495/1500, tempera on panel, National Gallery of Art, Washington, D.C., Widener Collection.

Image © Board of Trustees, National Gallery of Art, Washington.

FIGURE 2. Artemisia Gentileschi, *Judith and Maidservant with the Head of Holofernes*, c. 1625, oil on canvas, The Detroit Institute of Arts, Gift of Mr. Leslie H. Green.

Photograph © 1984 The Detroit Institute of Arts.

The beheading of Holofernes was a popular subject in Renaissance and baroque Italy because Judith could represent both personal valor and civic triumph. Although both pictures contain many of the same narrative elements, and each artist aggrandizes the heroine by making her large in scale and placing her close to the viewer's own space, they ultimately offer very different versions of the story and its female protagonist. The Renaissance interpretation of this theme by Mantegna (or follower) gives us a stoic, timeless, and cerebral heroine who is as cool as a cucumber, while Gentileschi casts her as furtive and poised for action, emphasizing the tale's tension and drama.

The earlier painting shows Judith standing victorious outside the darkened tent, her face impassive as she prepares to drop Holofernes' head into the open sack and escape the enemy camp. The general's severed head—highly visible against the vibrant orange of her servant Abra's robe—underscores Judith's power. Unlike Abra, Judith does not grimace at the gruesome trophy in her hand. She is idealized through classically inspired draperies and a graceful yet weighty, columnar pose. Her physical stature is accentuated by the strong vertical of the tent pole and through contrast with the stooping posture of her maidservant. The tent draperies frame Judith like a heraldic cloth of honor while creating a stable, pyramidal composition that lends the picture an immutable and timeless aura. The colors are clear, bright, and weighted in the primaries, which contribute to the picture's overall suggestion of a carefully deliberated and rational act.

Gentileschi's version is more dramatic and suspenseful. Judith and her servant are in Holofernes' tent. The fatal blow has just been struck, and they are interrupted as Abra tries to stuff the head into the sack. Her hand outstretched cautioning *silence!*, sword poised for their defense, Judith looks up, alert to impending danger just beyond the frame and the spectator's field of vision. Gentileschi's Judith is a flesh and blood woman, solid, weighty, fully capable of wielding the sword and decapitating her foe. She grips her weapon with serious intent, unlike her Renaissance counterpart who holds hers as if it were a fashion accessory. The harsh, theatrical lighting conveys the drama and tension surrounding this moment of possible discovery. The diagonal thrust of Gentileschi's composition, from lower right to upper left, created by the illuminated bodies of the women, augments the image's dynamic visual power.

These pictures tell the same story but use different visual ingredients; pictorially, they are worlds apart. As a result of the choices each artist made, the paintings offer radically different psychologies of the events depicted—one rational and cool, the other more dramatic and emotional. What is important to note is that the fullness of the story cannot be separated from the means of its telling.

A comparison of two Italian Renaissance portraits of affluent young women is equally illustrative (Figures 3 and 4). Both depict their subjects at the advent of their married lives—the principal occasion for a lady's portrait. Both are approximately the same half-length format (although the Leonardo has suffered the loss of the lower part of the picture, which originally may have included the sitter's hands). Both are painted in a subdued palette dominated by earth tones.

Without delving into the symbolism of these pictures, or the ways portraiture of this period differs from what we are familiar with today, there are certain visual cues that convey distinctly different messages about the women—messages that transcend barriers of time and cultural context. The portrait of Bianca Maria Sforza is primarily a picture about the social status of the bride, whose lavish jewels and richly brocaded dress are minutely described. Costume, in fact, is given prominence over the sitter herself, whose profile placement against a neutral background effectively isolates her from the viewer and underscores her privileged social position. The portrait of Ginevra de' Benci is much more a study in individual psychology. Ginevra's costume is relatively simple and unadorned, blending into the background. Her three-quarter pose fully reveals her pensive face, while her gaze steadily meets the spectator's.

As these examples reveal, every picture tells a story. The key is learning how to decode a picture's visual language—a skill that can be applied to the appreciation of fine art as well as to the more mundane images and visual information that bombard us daily. To become fluent in this skill is to become *visually literate.* Not unlike written and oral

FIGURE 3. Leonardo da Vinci, *Ginevra de' Benci,* c. 1474, oil on panel, National Gallery of Art, Washington, D.C., Ailsa Mellon Bruce Fund.

literacies, visual literacy involves learning a system of symbols and cues. However, while a symbol system such as language is typically used to convey specific meanings in as straightforward and unambiguous a manner as possible, the artist's system of visual symbol-making is used more evocatively and metaphorically to convey multiple levels of meaning. The poet's use of language, which is aesthetic and connotative rather than purely denotative, perhaps offers the closest parallel to the painter's visual mode of communication (Gardner, 1990).

Visual literacy will only gain importance in our multimedia age and should be recognized as a unique learning modality—one that complements the traditionally sanctioned verbal and mathematical intelligences. Visual learning should also be given a more prominent place in contemporary education because it draws heavily upon the emotional aspects of cognition.

Intellect and emotion—the twin engines of learning—are typically presented as polar opposites. The rational/logical side of learning has traditionally dominated pedagogy, while the affective side of learning has always been held in lower regard, if not ignored altogether. Yet the role of the emotions in learning has lately assumed new importance in research and learning theory. Eric Jensen (1998, p. 71) points out, "The affective side of learning is the critical interplay between how we feel, act, and think. There is no separation of mind and emotions; emotions, thinking, and learning are all linked." While noting that extremes of emotions are counterproductive in the classroom, Jensen argues that they have a legitimate place in education and even advocates organizing classroom instruction around activities and topics that engage students on a very personal level.

FIGURE 4. Ambrogio de Predis, *Bianca Maria Sforza,* probably 1493, oil on panel, National Gallery of Art, Washington, D.C., Widener Collection.

Music, games, dramatic performance, and storytelling are all activities that require students to give deeply of themselves. Assignments that involve debate and dialogue, journaling, and other forms of personal reflection also help foster learning through feeling. As Jenson puts it, "Good learning does not avoid emotions, it embraces them."

Images are important conduits for affective learning. Artistic images, in particular, make their greatest appeal to our emotions and give shape to our inner experiences. As any teacher of elementary or middle school can attest, visual art captures a child's imagination, whether she is looking at a picture or creating her own. Art is a uniquely personal experience—and one that offers respite from the more traditional classroom activities. A picture can easily become the point of departure for creative writing or storytelling. The combination of image and word has broad educational applications for students at all grade levels.

Why Storytelling with Digital Images?

STORIES–VISUAL and verbal–are powerful vehicles for affective learning. Penninah Schram notes that one of the primary ways we build community with others is by sharing stories: "Storytelling connects people. It connects hearts. It helps answer questions like: Who am I? Who are my people? With what values did they live? How should I live? How should I die? What are the legacies that I want to transmit to my children and to the next generation?" (as quoted in Mooney & Holt, 1996, p. 8).

The pedagogical dimensions of storytelling in the classroom might be summarized as follows (Schank, 1995):

- *Humanistic:* Storytelling is a culturally rich and venerated practice that is global in relevance and encourages people to value their experiences–imaginary or real. Stories put us in touch with ourselves and with others, and communicate values.

- *Cross-disciplinary:* Storytelling applies to many school subjects, particularly in language arts and social studies.

- *Cross-cultural:* Narrative structures cut across cultural and geographic spaces.

- *Multisensory, multimodal:* Storytelling is visual, auditory, and kinesthetic, and unites verbal and technological literacies.

- *Constructivist:* Storytelling is learner-centered; tales are created out of an individual's knowledge and experience.

- *Memory and narrative:* We learn in story structures and think in terms of stories.

Digital storytelling–using a computer equipped with electronic text and imaging software to tell tales–is but a contemporary canvas for an age-old art form. It allows many of the traditional elements of performance-based storytelling to become seamlessly integrated–the visual and verbal, the kinesthetic and auditory–by using a platform familiar and appealing to today's youth. The computer is the new campfire around which students gather and interact.

Because digital storytelling integrates a wide range of tasks–including scriptwriting and editing, image manipulation, voice-over narration, music selection, and timing–it allows teachers to address multiple learning styles within a single project. Because it draws on a wide range of academic skills, it has great cross-curricular potential.

Digital storytelling also allows students to build technical skills required in an increasingly complex, electronic society, and readily addresses the National Educational Technology Standards for Students. As students learn word processing and imaging software, or transfer video clips and still photographs from digital cameras to computers for use in electronic movies, they master general technology concepts and operational skills.

Among master teachers, digital storytelling is rapidly becoming a major vehicle for building 21ˢᵗ-century literacies. According to Kathleen Tyner (1998), author of *Literacy in a Digital World,* electronic storytelling offers the advantages of an experiential approach to learning, while combining oral and written literacies with those intrinsic to the new multimedia.

Digital Storytelling at the National Gallery of Art

IN 2003 and 2004, the educational potential of digital storytelling was explored in a National Gallery of Art program entitled *Storytelling and the Visual Arts.* Teachers from all disciplines participated in an intense three-day workshop, during which they developed a short three- to five-minute digital movie that focused on an artistic motif of their choice. Teachers arrived at the workshop with a one-page script and a dozen images. With ready access to digital cameras, digital image editing software, and Macintosh computers, these teachers quickly identified digital storytelling as an effective educational medium.

The tutorial was led by Joe Lambert, director of the Center for Digital Storytelling in Berkeley, California. The center's Web site (www.storycenter.org) provides a step-by-step description of the digital storytelling process and a representative range of final stories produced at workshops conducted around the United States and abroad.

Digital storytelling is a compelling and satisfying process; it begins with crafting the right story and continues through the digitally mediated editing, rendering, and presentation stages. It is learner-centered in the best way imaginable, in that it asks us to make meaning out of experience *we deem significant.* There is also the "me" element—the movie is all about its maker. For once we can say, with full impunity from any accusations of raging ego, "It's all about *me!*" This can offer a particularly powerful way for student authors to find their voice.

Digital storytelling, as practiced by those collaborating with the Gallery, is both *about* art and an art form in itself. After creating their own digital stories, teachers are better equipped to coach their students through the same process. Many young people never encounter visual art at home, and even in school they may fail to connect personally to the objects their teachers have chosen for study. But if allowed to choose art that speaks to them and conveys the essence of their own story, they find that imagery can become a powerful catalyst for self-expression.

Onnie, a high school studio art teacher from New Jersey, created a potent model for his students in *Renaissance Memory*—a story of art, family history, and the Harlem

Renaissance. The image that launched his journey of personal discovery was Palmer Hayden's *The Janitor Who Paints* (Figure 5).

As the narrative unfolds, it is clear the painting speaks to Onnie's own identity as an artist and the legacy of those dreamers and "strivers" who came before him:

PALMER HAYDEN'S *The Janitor Who Paints* brings together all of the feelings that I had about art. The artist sits next to a trash can, intently studying a pretty young mother and her baby. All three are proud to be who they are. Even in a basement, they are all obviously strivers. Around the room are the tools of both of Palmer Hayden's trades; the broom and the feather duster are as important as the canvas and the easel. He wears a beret cocked to the side, a symbol of an artist. It is also the hat that Dizzy Gillespie and Harlem hipsters wore to top off their zoot suits.

I recognize my father and my uncles in all of them. *The Janitor Who Paints* is like all those strivers who came north to become the heroes of the next generation.

Smithsonian American Art Museum, Gift of the Harmon Foundation.

FIGURE 5. Palmer Hayden, *The Janitor Who Paints*, c. 1937, oil on canvas, Smithsonian American Art Museum, Washington, D.C.

FIGURE 6. South German (Swabian or Franconian), *The Holy Kinship,* c. 1480/1490, painted wood, National Gallery of Art, Washington, D.C., Patron's Permanent Fund.

Tom, a high school arts resource teacher from Maryland, crafted an equally moving tale wrought with difficult and determined self-examination. For his electronic story, he chose to examine a late-medieval devotional sculpture depicting the Christ child surrounded by members of his extended family (Figure 6). The rich colors and brilliantly reflective gold-leaf surfaces give the sculpture a jewel-like, regal quality that underscores the importance of the religious subject. Gestures and facial expressions are exquisitely rendered and run the gamut of human emotions.

Interestingly, when Tom read his script out loud to the group, his words were neutral, distant, and documentary-like—completely at odds with the image he chose and the overall project goal of exploring one's personal responses to a work of art. With coaching, Tom stepped back and reconsidered his source of inspiration.

Tom revised his story into an insightful, personal reflection on what struck him most about the sculpture, reactions he was at first unable to articulate. Chief among them were the range of emotions displayed by each man and woman in the presence of the Christ child and the power relationships between genders, suggested by the placement of men and women within the sculptural tableau. Family photographs from Tom's own childhood were interwoven with his reflections on the artwork and the gender relations depicted, including reminiscences about household role models with whom he grew up.

Tom's story took him on a journey from head to heart, in which historical facts and objective visual data become inflected with personal meanings and associations. What started as a scholarly exegesis developed into something deeper, triggering the powerful memories, values, and truths that are at the core of the best stories. He found his voice and took ownership of the artwork. History was supplanted by *his* story—Tom's. As both Tom's and Onnie's experiences suggest, everyone, and every picture, has a story to tell.

The challenge for teachers in schools is to add this powerful mode of self-expression to their inventory of pedagogical strategies and tools, and to employ it to address curricular goals. The content area chapters provide examples of ways this can be accomplished in different classrooms. The goal is to effectively communicate content in a manner that empowers the learner. Visual imagery offers an effective mechanism for achieving this, and the new technologies available to teachers offer new opportunities for introducing imagery into the classroom.

Web Resources of the National Gallery of Art

THIS SECTION provides an annotated list of National Gallery of Art Web sites educators may mine for ideas and images.

National Gallery of Art
www.nga.gov
> A wide range of digital images and teaching resources for K–12 educators are available at the National Gallery of Art's Web site. The home page links directly to the Division of Education's lists of programs and offerings. Of particular interest for teachers are the following Gallery Web addresses.

NGA Classroom
www.nga.gov/education/classroom/index.htm
> NGA Classroom is the main Gallery Web site for teachers wishing to integrate art into the curriculum. It features online lessons for teachers and interactives for students that extend selected lessons, allowing students to make their own mobiles, for example, or learn more about the gods and goddesses of Greco-Roman antiquity. A resource finder allows a search for Gallery online teaching materials by curriculum topic, art subject, or artist's name.

NGA Loan Materials
www.nga.gov/education/classroom/loanfinder
> This teaching resource finder complements NGA Classroom and allows a search for loan materials that can be ordered online and direct-mailed for classroom use. Materials can be searched by curriculum topic, art subject, or artist's name. Particular formats can be specified: teaching packet with slides, CD-ROM, DVD, videodisc, and video.

NGA Kids
www.nga.gov/kids/kids.htm
> This is the Gallery's Web site for children, with interactive art-making projects at the Art Zone, featuring online collage and portrait-making projects, among others.

Digital Image Database and Search Engine
www.nga.gov/search
> Text or data on all of the more than 108,000 objects in the Gallery's collection can be found using various search capabilities. Images of more than 5,600 objects in the collection are available. Search by artist's name, object title, or by keywords and phrases. Check **images only** to limit your search to objects for which images are available.

Resources for More Information

Bull, G., Bull, G., Thomas, J., & Jordan, J. (2000). Incorporating imagery into instruction. *Learning and Leading with Technology, 27*(6), 46-49, 63.

Consortium of National Arts Education Associations. (1994). *The National standards for art education*. Retrieved February 10, 2005, from **http://artsedge.kennedy-center.org/teach/standards/**

Freedberg, D. (1989). *The power of images: Studies in the history and theory of response*. Chicago: University of Chicago.

Gardner, H. (1985). *Frames of mind: The theory of multiple intelligences*. New York: HarperCollins.

Gardner, H. (1990). *Art education and human development*. Santa Monica, CA: Getty Center for Education in the Arts.

International Society for Technology in Education. (2000). *National educational technology standards for students: Connecting curriculum and technology*. Eugene, OR: Author. Also available online at **http://cnets.iste.org/students/s_book.html**

Jensen, E. (1998). *Teaching with the brain in mind*. Alexandria, VA: Association for Supervision and Curriculum Development.

Lambert, J. (2002). *Digital storytelling: Capturing lives, creating community*. Berkeley, CA: Digital Diner Press.

Mooney, B., & Holt, D. (1996). *The storyteller's guide*. Little Rock, AR: August House.

Schank, R. C. (1995). *Tell me a story: Narrative and intelligence*. Evanston, IL: Northwestern University Press.

Shahn, B. (1957). *The shape of content*. Cambridge, MA: Harvard University Press.

Stafford, B. M. (1996). *Good looking: Essays on the virtue of images.* Cambridge, MA: MIT Press.

Tyner, K. (1998). *Literacy in a digital world: Teaching and learning in the age of information.* Mahwah, NJ: Lawrence Erlbaum.

West, T. G. (1997). *In the mind's eye: Visual thinkers, gifted people with dyslexia and other learning difficulties, computer images and the ironies of creativity* (Rev. ed.). Amherst, NY: Prometheus.

White, M. A. (1987). *Information and imagery education: What curriculum for the Information Age?* Hillsdale, NJ: Lawrence Erlbaum.

PART 2

using
digital images
across the
curriculum

CHAPTER 6

John C. Park and
Randy L. Bell

digital images
in the science classroom

IN MANY ways, visualization is more fundamental to science teaching than it is to any of the other core content areas. Many natural processes—and even some objects—are too small, too fast, too slow, or too far away to view without highly specialized equipment, and must be illustrated in the classroom using various visualization tools. Teachers have long known that students at every grade level understand scientific concepts better when they can see the phenomenon they are studying. That is why science textbooks are full of illustrations, photographs, and diagrams, and science teachers stock their classrooms with microscopes. Teachers regularly use videotapes and DVDs to present a wide variety of visual images to students, and the World Wide Web has opened access to even more up-to-the-minute, state-of-the-art scientific images.

Opportunities for Visualizing Science

TODAY'S NEW technologies for capturing, processing, displaying, and analyzing images have opened new opportunities for visualization in the science classroom—placing control of image-making in the hands of teachers and students. This chapter begins by identifying some of the new digital imaging technologies that are easy to use and appropriate for acquiring, analyzing, creating, and communicating images in the science classroom. Then it describes a number of classroom-tested activities that integrate digital images in the areas of life science, physical science, Earth science, and space science.

ACQUIRE

Digital imaging devices were once the sole domain of scientists, but technological advances have made them readily accessible to K–12 science classes. Today's digital imaging devices include still cameras (including flex cams and Web cams), video cameras, and digital microscopes.

Digital cameras are more compact than traditional film cameras yet typically offer a large image-storing capacity. Picture quality and resolution continue to increase; some wallet-sized cameras can now capture 5 megapixel images. Digital cameras are so small and handy they can be taken anywhere, and are even becoming a common feature of cell phones. Scientific images of natural phenomena can be captured during a walk through the neighborhood or on a vacation.

The ubiquity of digital cameras means that thousands of images are generated every day, many of which can be used to explore scientific concepts. Digital cameras can also be used for recording and digitizing large documents such as maps, and for creating stop-motion movies. Newer digital cameras typically have the capability to record short videos, and full-featured digital video cameras are becoming increasingly available to many classrooms. Video cameras allow students to record natural phenomenon involving movement for later observation and analysis. Two activities in this chapter, "Life in a Bird's Nest" and "Investigating a Solar Eclipse," use a digital video camera.

Microscopes are one of the most common instructional tools used in the science classroom, but conventional microscopes have several well-documented limitations. Students have trouble focusing microscopes, and because each person's eyes are different, there is no easy way for a teacher to check students' focusing skills. Students often confuse key components of images viewed under a microscope, mistaking a magnified speck of dust, for example, for an anatomical feature. Students can spend an entire class period looking at air bubbles instead of the organisms they are supposed to be observing. Consequently, much of a teacher's instructional time is spent trying to ensure that students are seeing what they should be seeing. Moreover, students have no way of capturing and sharing what they see.

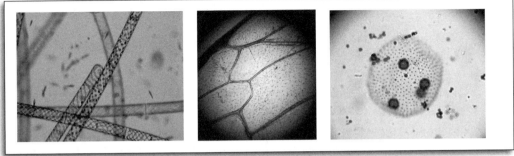

Photographs by Douglas Toti.

FIGURE 1. Images captured with a digital camera and compound microscope. From left: spyrogyra (100x), a bee's wing (40x), and volvox (100x).

Digital microscopes, on the other hand, allow students to project images on a computer monitor or movie screen and highlight features or phenomena of interest. Students can capture still or even moving images for later analysis (see Figure 1).

Many of today's digital cameras can be directly connected to existing school microscopes. As long as the camera is threaded for interchangeable lenses, it can be fitted with an adapter to attach it to a microscope (see Figure 2). Firms such as Scopetronix (**www.scopetronix.com**) provide adapters for many different makes and models of digital cameras. This approach to digital image acquisition allows schools to build upon and extend existing resources.

Camera photograph by Douglas Toti; microscope photograph by Lynn Bell.

FIGURE 2. At left is a digital camera attached to a compound microscope. At right is the Intel QX3 digital microscope.

In addition to retrofitting existing microscopes, teachers and students can purchase digital microscopes designed specifically for educational use. The Intel QX3 was one of the first such digital microscopes to be used extensively in science classrooms (see Figure 2).

Digital microscopes can be both affordable and easy to use. The Intel QX3 is so easy to use, in fact, it was originally designed and marketed as a toy. Although Intel eventually stopped producing the QX3, Digital Blue (**http://playdigitalblue.com/products/qx3/ info/**) observed how teachers were using it in schools and adapted and remarketed it with teaching guides that provide curriculum activities linked to science education standards. Other manufacturers have followed Digital Blue's lead.

Several digital microscopes and some cameras (such as the Canon A-series cameras) include time-lapse capabilities that can be useful both when coupled with a microscope and when used directly for data collection. Images captured through time-lapse photography and stored in a digital format can be played back as a digital movie. Students can then watch the process again and again in faster-than-real time, or stop it at any point to make observations or measurements.

Two of the activities described in this chapter, "Metamorphosis of a Butterfly" and "Crystal Growth," use time-lapse photography. When science students acquire and analyze images of this kind, they gain a deeper understanding of scientific processes that would otherwise not be visible.

ANALYZE

The image of the smoke trail from a space shuttle launch (see Figure 3) demonstrates that visual evidence of scientific concepts can be found anywhere if we train students to look closely enough. Teachers can pose a number of questions to students based on examination of this image (a color version is available on the CD accompanying this book):

- Why is there a color difference in the sky just above the horizon in comparison with the sky at the top of the image?

- The exhaust plume near the horizon is a dark red, while the plume at higher altitudes appears to be white. What would cause this?

The explanation for both questions lies in the concept of differential dispersion of blue light by tiny particles in the atmosphere, the same phenomenon that causes red sunsets (see **www.weatherquestions.com/Why_are_sunsets_red.htm** for a concise explanation).

- Why is the exhaust plume bent in the middle?

The exhaust plume in Figure 3 clearly reveals that wind speeds differ depending on altitude. Scientific data are not always numeric; this example illustrates how images can be used to promote qualitative inquiry.

Photograph by John C. Park.

FIGURE 3. A shot taken minutes after the launch of the space shuttle Discovery on March 8, 2001, using default camera settings.

Analyzing digital images can also help students overcome misconceptions. For example, many students have difficulty recognizing that plants—like animals—are alive, because plants do not move in the manner of other living organisms. Time-lapse videos of plant growth (e.g., a seed sprouting or a vine twining itself around a branch) can make the abstract concept of plant movement directly observable and more concrete.

The Geometer's Sketchpad is a program from Key Curriculum Press (**www.keypress.com**) that allows users to create geometric sketches that are very useful in the quantitative analysis of images. When an image is pasted into the Sketchpad work area, the software provides the necessary tools to make many kinds of measurements. The "Measuring the Moon" activity in this chapter uses the Geometer's Sketchpad.

CREATE

Contrary to what many students believe, the scientific endeavor involves a great deal of intuition and creativity, especially when researchers are synthesizing data and drawing conclusions from the information. As students try to make sense of visual data, they will rely heavily on their inferencing skills and knowledge of scientific principles to *create* a reasonable explanation. Students use knowledge gained from their observation and analysis of digital images to create new explanations that can solidify their understanding of scientific principles.

The Butterfly Project (developed by preservice teacher Ann Bowen) is an excellent example of how digital photography can engender student creativity in a biology class (Bowen & Bell, 2004). Rather than having her students spend 15 minutes reading from a textbook about the butterfly life cycle, Bowen directed students to observe real butterflies over the course of their life cycle, capturing the metamorphosis with digital cameras and microscopes. Students came up with creative ways to capture life cycle events and figure out why and what was happening. This technology-aided exploration of a natural process required students to engage their creativity, intuition, and scientific knowledge in profoundly memorable ways.

CONTENT STANDARDS

The National Science Education Standards are sponsored by the National Research Council, **www.nap.edu/ readingroom/books/ nses/html/.**

COMMUNICATE

The scientific process consists not only of discovery but also of the communication of findings through publication, a process that can be greatly enhanced with the inclusion of digital images. Most word processors now include annotation features that also allow images and graphics to be labeled.

Students increasingly maintain electronic portfolios of their work. When an electronic portfolio is posted on the Web, parents may easily view and follow their children's work. This medium also facilitates inclusion of multimedia elements, such as a video clip of a butterfly emerging from a chrysalis or digital movies of saltwater evaporating.

The following activities are examples of the knowledge that can be constructed by science teachers and students using the latest digital imaging tools.

Life in a Bird's Nest
Life Science
GRADE LEVELS: K–8

Objectives

- Students will investigate and search for patterns of behavior of recently hatched robins and of their parents.

- Students will generate possible explanations for such behavior.

NETS·S Addressed

5. Technology research tools

- Students use technology to locate, evaluate, and collect information from a variety of sources.

- Students use technology tools to process data and report results.

National Science Education Standards Addressed

- Content Standard A (K–4, 5–8): All students should develop abilities necessary to do scientific inquiry.

- Content Standard C (K–4): All students should develop understanding of the characteristics of organisms, the life cycles of organisms, and organisms and their environments.

- Content Standard C (5–8): All students should develop understanding of reproduction and heredity, regulation and behavior, and diversity and adaptations of organisms.

Materials Needed

video camera and tripod

plenty of videotape for long-term capturing of images

Web Resources

All About Birds (Cornell Lab of Ornithology)
http://birds.cornell.edu/programs/AllAboutBirds/BirdGuide/American_Robin_dtl.html
  An amazing Web site that includes information about various types of birds, including bird songs.

American Robin
www.learner.org/jnorth/spring2004/robin/Update042704.html
  Provides an abundance of information about robins. The "Scoop on Poop" lesson is quite interesting.

Project Nest Watch
www.bsc-eoc.org/national/nw_finding.html
  This Web site gives assistance to the user in locating and monitoring bird nests. The site also provides other useful information about the American robin.

Activities

HOW MANY times do we see things happening in the natural world but have little specific knowledge about it? For example, when birds build a nest and lay eggs, do both parents take care of the brood? What must be done to bring the brood to independence? What happens in that nest?

ACQUIRE

Look for opportunities to capture phenomena in their natural context: for example, a pair of robins building a nest nearby. The images in Figure 4 were taken by author John Park from his dining room window. The robins did not seem to be affected by his attention; he was able to shoot 13 hours of digital video over the course of several days, documenting the birth and growth of the hatchlings until the final bird left the nest.

ANALYZE

To make it easier for students to sift through all the data, teachers should edit the documentary video and select only the most important events in the nest. A series of questions should be developed to guide the students in their observations. This is a good time for students to practice basic science process skills. The students should review the edited tapes to classify tasks for both the parents and brood. Tasks for the brood might include resting, waiting, eating, defecating, preening, and exercising. Tasks for the parents might include obtaining food, feeding the brood, cleaning the nest, cleaning each chick, removing debris from the nest, protecting the nest, and resting. Students could view the images to find out how much time is spent on each activity and discuss why each event is important.

Questions for students to research using the teacher-prepared digital video could include:

1. Do one or both parents take care of the brood?

2. What is the average time that the brood is left alone?

3. How do the chicks lose their fuzz?

4. What is that bag of white stuff that the parents remove from the back of each chick?

5. When do the chicks know that their parents are in the area? Is it different when they are young compared with when they are older?

6. What do the parents provide for the chicks to eat?

7. On one day four chicks were in the nest. The next day the nest held only three. What may have happened to the fourth chick?

Photographs by John C. Park.

FIGURE 4. At left is a clip showing two robins attending the brood. The clip in the right shows a parent removing a white sack from the backside of one of the chicks.

CREATE

Students should organize their observations and search for patterns in the data. Have them classify the behaviors they observe for both the chicks and the parents. These behaviors could be placed in a data table as headers. Frequencies of the behaviors can be tallied in the tables. Use the questions in the previous section to investigate relationships among the behaviors.

COMMUNICATE

What is the purpose for the observed behaviors of the chicks and parents? After the students have completed their observations and searched for patterns of behavior, engage the students in discussing the purpose of each behavior. For example, when the students notice that the parents spend much time cleaning the nest, ask why this is important. What might happen if the waste is allowed to stay in the nest? This could be done in small groups and then the results could be shared in the larger class environment.

MODIFICATIONS

Have students set up a video camera to record animal or insect behavior, such as the class pet (especially during the night), a spider in a web, fish in a tank, or monkeys at a zoo.

Metamorphosis of a Butterfly
Life Science
GRADE LEVELS: 4–8

Objective

■ Students will observe the life cycle of the butterfly, particularly chrysalis formation and the emergence of the adult.

NETS·S Addressed

4. Technology communications tools

- Students use a variety of media and formats to communicate information and ideas effectively to multiple audiences.

5. Technology research tools

- Students use technology tools to process data and report results.

National Science Education Standards Addressed

■ Content Standard A (K–4, 5–8): All students should develop abilities necessary to do scientific inquiry.

■ Content Standard C (K–4): All students should develop understanding of the characteristics of organisms, the life cycles of organisms, and organisms and their environments.

■ Content Standard C (5–8): All students should develop understanding of reproduction and heredity.

Materials Needed

camera or digital microscope with time-lapse capabilities, such as the QX3 digital microscope

tripod

Painted Lady Classroom Breeding Kit or equivalent

software for creating a movie, such as Movie Maker, iMovie, Pinnacle Studio, or QuickTime Pro

Web Resources

All About Painted Lady Butterflies
www.earthsbirthday.org/butterflies/activitykit/2.html
    The title says it all.

The Butterfly Site.com
www.thebutterflysite.com/biology.shtml
    This site describes butterfly biology, raising painted lady butterflies, and the migration of monarch butterflies. It also offers many links to other butterfly sites.

CameraScope
www.teacherlink.org/tools/
    This site offers free software that lets you connect your digital camera to a computer and control the image capture.

Activities

MANY LIFE science events occur gradually over a long period of time. A young observer viewing the event for 15 minutes may not notice any changes at all during that time. However, if images are captured at regular intervals over time, a time-lapse movie can be constructed of the event, condensing a day's worth of activity into a few seconds of viewing.

Many elementary school classes raise painted lady butterflies to help students better understand the concept of the life cycle. Unfortunately, some of the most fascinating steps in the process—chrysalis formation and the emergence of the butterfly—happen very slowly or when students are not in the classroom. Time-lapse photography can catch these events and record them for further observation and analysis.

ACQUIRE

Older students can be given the task of figuring out how to set up the digital imaging device for photographing a caterpillar or chrysalis. Younger students will need more guidance.

A device that can be set to capture images automatically at regular intervals over several hours is ideal for this activity. The QX3 digital microscope (set on its lowest magnification) is one tool that has this capability and is easy for students to use. Some digital cameras have a built-in time-lapse mode setting, or you may be able to connect your digital camera to a computer and control the image capture using software such as CameraScope, available for free download at **www.teacherlink.org/tools/**.

The camera or digital microscope should be placed on a sturdy tripod. If the camera has an adjustable lens, make sure it is set on wide angle. The same distance and lens setting should be used for each photograph. The "macro" setting on the camera may provide the best close-up focus. On some cameras, a flower icon indicates the macro focus setting. Once the camera is set, it should not be moved at any time during the image capturing, not even between photographs.

It is possible to capture images manually, but the teacher or student must be available when the event begins and must remain with the camera during the entire event. In this case, it is best to capture the image using a remote control device (either a wired or infrared remote), because any movement of the camera will be noticeable in the resulting movie. To get a good movie of a chrysalis forming or a butterfly emerging, images should be captured about every 15 seconds (see Figure 5 for a still image taken from a time-lapse film clip). The process goes so quickly that you will miss much of it if the capture period is longer.

CREATE AND ANALYZE

The images will need to be processed into a movie before the observer can view the time-lapse event. There are several ways to create a movie out of a set of images. If you are

Photograph by Randy Bell.

FIGURE 5. A monarch butterfly just after it emerged from its chrysalis.

using a QX3 digital microscope, the software that comes with the microscope makes the process quick and easy. Most video editing programs (such as Movie Maker, iMovie, or Pinnacle Studio) can do the same. Another widely available software package—QuickTime Pro—can also assemble a movie out of a set of digital still images. While the free QuickTime Player can be downloaded to any computer, QuickTime Pro gives you many additional features at a minimal cost (see sidebar for tips on using QuickTime for this activity).

Generate questions based on what appears in the time-lapse movie. Use these questions for directed student inquiry as they interact with the movie using the standard digital video controller. For example, once the butterfly emerges from the chrysalis, why does it not immediately begin to flutter? What is required before flying can occur? How does this process occur?

CREATE AND COMMUNICATE

Some students may make observations that other students do not notice. Using a single image from the time-lapse movie, let the students create a printed page of that image along with a description of that specific observation. Put the observation descriptions and images on the wall for each student to read and critique.

MODIFICATION

To read about one teacher's classroom experience doing a butterfly project with digital cameras and microscopes, go to **www.teacherlink.org/content/science/class_examples/home.html**.

The Need for Speed
Physical Science
GRADE LEVELS: 4–8

Objective

■ Students will discover the two factors determining average speed: the change of distance and the change in time.

NETS·S Addressed

1. Basic operations and concepts

- Students demonstrate a sound understanding of the nature and operation of technology systems.
- Students are proficient in the use of technology.

3. Technology productivity tools

- Students use technology tools to enhance learning, increase productivity, and promote creativity.

6. Technology problem-solving and decision-making tools

- Students use technology resources for solving problems and making informed decisions.

National Science Education Standards Addressed

■ Content Standard A (K–4, 5–8): All students should develop abilities necessary to do scientific inquiry. All students should develop understandings about scientific inquiry.

■ Content Standard B (K–4): All students should develop an understanding of position and motion of objects.

■ Content Standard B (5–8): All students should develop an understanding of motions and forces.

Materials Needed

meter stick or paper with graduated lines

two cars of different colors

camera mounted high on a tripod that looks down on a table or floor

software that will convert images into a movie, such as QuickTime Pro

graphical analysis program, such as Logger Pro

Web Resource

Physics Teaching and Learning Videos
www.cabrillo.edu/academics/physics/videos.html
This site includes sample videos using the stroboscope technique. Unlike stop-motion animation (which is made up of many separate still images that are spliced together), stroboscopic videos use a strobe light source that operates while the camera lens remains open, exposing moments of motion on the film.

Activities

TWO OF the earliest films featuring stop-motion animation were by Willis O'Brien (*The Lost World,* 1925; *King Kong,* 1933). Ray Harryhausen was another early developer of modern stop-motion animation techniques, with movies such as *Mighty Joe Young* (1949) and *The Seventh Voyage of Sinbad* (1958). Using the same techniques these film pioneers used (but with digital camera technology), students can make their own educational epics!

ACQUIRE

Stop-motion animation is accomplished by creating a "stage" of characters and capturing a sequence of images, moving the characters slightly between each image. This maneuvering can be quite a challenge to control for complex scenes such as those in movies, but the scenes your students create can be much simpler.

Place a distance reference of 0 cm to at least 48 cm (using a meter stick or tape with marks) on the top of the table that will be used as a stage. Students should set the digital camera on a tripod and make sure the whole scene fits on the LCD screen, with the camera lens set on wide angle. They should place two toy cars of different colors (yellow and red, for the purposes of this discussion) at the 0 cm mark and capture an image. They then should move the yellow car forward 1 cm and the red car forward 2 cm and capture another image. This sequence should continue with students moving the cars forward at the same corresponding intervals and capturing an image each time. By the time 24 images are captured, the yellow car should be nearing the 24 cm mark and the red car should be near the 48 cm mark. They should now have 24 sequential images captured in the camera to download to the computer (see Figure 6 for three sample frames).

> **ANIMATION TIP**
>
> For best stop-motion animation, make small changes between captured images.

CREATE AND ANALYZE

The method for creating a movie out of the sequence of images is precisely the same as that used for time-lapse photography. Use software that will convert the set of images into a movie. QuickTime Pro does this quite well, having the advantage that the user can easily modify the frame rate. Initially, have students set the frame rate at 24 frames per second. Ask students, "Since the movie consists of 24 images, how long should the movie last?"

As they watch the movie, ask students which car appears to be moving faster. Since one car moves twice the distance in the same amount of time, it is moving faster. How fast? The slower car moved a total of 24 cm in one second, so the average speed of that car is 24 cm/s. What is the average speed of the faster car?

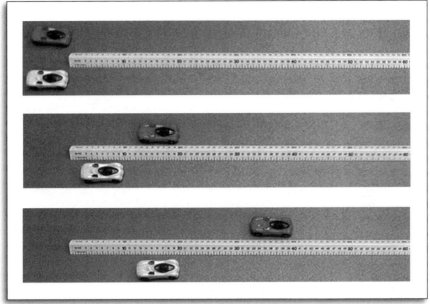

FIGURE 6. Frames 1, 11, and 21 of the constant velocity movie.

Challenge students by asking them how they could make the cars appear to move faster without recapturing the stop-motion animation. If they created another movie with the same set of images but using a different frame rate, would they need to increase the frames per second or decrease the frames per second? Students should try it both ways to see what happens. By doing this activity, students will see that there are two factors that determine the rate at which an object moves: the distance the object travels, and the amount of time required to move that distance.

With older students, this activity could be expanded to investigate objects whose velocity is not constant. For example, students could create a similar movie in which the yellow car starts out at 1 cm increments and the red car starts out at 2 cm increments. When the yellow car hits the 12 cm mark, however, it gradually accelerates until it reaches an increment of 4 cm. Have students determine how many new frames will be needed before the two cars are even again.

CREATE AND COMMUNICATE

Have groups of students create a stop-motion animation movie of a car moving in a straight line. Include a meter stick for a reference. Tell the students to use QuickTime to create a movie from the images at a frame rate of 10 frames per second (each frame represents 0.1 second). After the movies are made, have the groups trade their movies so the other groups can create a distance-time graph of the motion using a graphical analysis program such as Logger Pro by Vernier Software and Technology. How would the graphs change if the movie was created with a QuickTime frame rate of 20 frames per second, but it was assumed that each frame represented a time of 0.1 second?

TIPS ON USING QUICKTIME PLAYER

Open QuickTime Player, go to File, and open the image sequence. Find the folder of images that you have captured, select the first image, and click to open it. A pop-up menu will appear asking you to adjust your frame viewing rate. The selections range from 60 frames per second to 10 seconds for each frame. To see a movie without flicker, select 24 frames per second or higher. Then, give your movie a title and save or run it.

MODIFICATION

After the students begin learning how to make adjustments in velocity, challenge them to create a stop-motion movie with the following scenario (enlisting a parent volunteer or other trusted adult): A person who is walking down the street is passed by a car traveling at a constant velocity. The person then speeds up and the car gradually slows to a stop until the person reaches the car. The person gets into the car, and the car uniformly speeds up until it reaches a constant velocity.

Crystal Growth
Physical Science
GRADE LEVELS: 5–8

Objective

■ Students will explore the effect of a solution's evaporation rate on crystal size.

NETS·S Addressed

5. Technology research tools

- Students use technology to locate, evaluate, and collect information from a variety of sources.

- Students use technology tools to process data and report results.

National Science Education Standards Addressed

■ Content Standard A (5–8): All students should develop abilities necessary to do scientific inquiry.

■ Content Standard B (5–8): All students should develop an understanding of properties and changes of properties in matter.

Materials Needed

digital microscope (or a digital camera attached to a traditional microscope using an adapter), and a connection to a computer with software that facilitates time-lapse photography

saturated salt solution (add salt to a small amount of hot water until no more will dissolve). Use the hot water for the fast evaporation slide. Let the solution cool to room temperature for the slow evaporation slide.

2 eyedroppers

2 microscope slides (no cover slip)

timer or clock

portable hairdryer or other warm air source

electronic slideshow or word processing software for viewing still images

presentation software for reports

Web Resources

Cycles
www.uen.org/themepark/cycles/rock.shtml
   A Utah site that includes basic information on rock cycles as well as online fieldtrips to geologically interesting sites, including Mount Saint Helens, the Grand Canyon, and Ayers Rock. The site is designed for the elementary level, but contains activities and links appropriate for all levels.

Molecular Expressions: Science Optics and You
http://micro.magnet.fsu.edu/optics/intelplay/intelanatomy.html
   This site offers detailed information on using the QX3 digital microscope and examples of its use in biology, geology, and chemistry.

National Mining Association Mining Education Site
www.nma.org/
> Part of the National Mining Association site is dedicated to mining education including educational materials, tour information for mines and mining museums around the United States, information on the adopt-a-school program for mining companies and schools, and other information on minerals and gems.

Rocks and the Rock Cycle
www.seismo.berkeley.edu/seismo/istat/9th/building_blocks.html#text
> Site developed to support the San Francisco Unified School curriculum project for ninth-grade Earth science. Includes rock cycle lessons and additional links to sites offering information on the rock cycle, minerals and gems, and classroom activities.

Activities

TRADITIONALLY, STUDENTS learn about differences in crystal size between intrusive and extrusive igneous rocks didactically through lecture and readings. Time-lapse photography of the process, on the other hand, enables students to discover for themselves the relationship between cooling time and crystal formation. Instead of perpetuating a learning situation in which students have typically been *told* the answers, using digital images to teach this process can do a great deal to promote student inquiry skills.

In this activity, students use a digital microscope (or a digital camera connected to a traditional microscope) to capture the fast and slow evaporation of saltwater. Through analysis of the time-lapse video clips, students identify differences in the size and appearance of the resulting salt crystal samples. Once students have learned the principle that larger crystals result from slower cooling, they can then apply this principle to predict the size of crystals resulting from rocks cooling quickly on the Earth's surface (extrusive) versus those forming from magma cooling slowly beneath the Earth's surface (intrusive).

ACQUIRE

Begin this activity by asking students: "How does the rate of evaporation of a drop of saltwater affect the resulting salt crystal formation?" For the slow evaporation, students can let a small drop of concentrated saltwater evaporate at room temperature (the larger the drop of water, the longer it will take to evaporate). For the fast evaporation, you will need to use hot saltwater and a blow dryer or other heat source to speed up the process (see the sidebar Capturing Crystal Formations for ideas on setting up this activity).

Using the microscope's low power, students should record images during the entire evaporation time. The time-lapse video should include images taken at regular intervals of 10–30 seconds. Before removing the slide, students should also capture a few still images of the crystals at different magnifications to facilitate comparison of the two results (see examples in Figure 7).

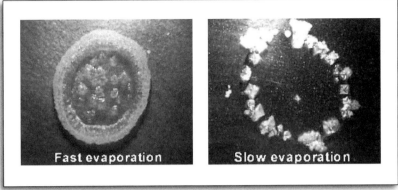

Photographs by Randy Bell.

FIGURE 7. Images of salt crystals formed during fast evaporation (left) and slow evaporation (right).

ANALYZE

The still images can be placed in an electronic slideshow or in a word processing document. Discuss the following questions with students:

- Are the crystals the same in both samples?

- What differences do you notice between the two final snapshots?

- What do you think caused this difference? [As the saltwater drops evaporate, the solubility of the salt in the water decreases, causing the salt to come out of the solution in the form of crystals. Crystals have less time to develop in a drop that evaporates quickly, resulting in smaller crystals.]

Have students use their observations to develop a conclusion about the crystals formed from the two drops of saltwater. The class will then be ready to discuss how crystals in igneous rocks are formed and the differences in structure between intrusive and extrusive igneous rocks.

CREATE

Promote a contest to see which team can design a system to create the largest crystals from an evaporated solution. The groups should develop hypotheses on the major variables that contribute to crystal size, create a system that incorporates those variables, and test their apparatus.

COMMUNICATE

The competition teams should take pictures of the resulting crystals and report to one another using presentation software. The resulting discussion should lead to ideas for building an apparatus to create a super-crystal.

MODIFICATIONS

If time is limited or you are working with younger students, you can prepare a time-lapse sequence ahead of time and show it to students using a projector. Along with the time-lapse video, slides of crystals formed at fast and slow evaporation rates may be prepared in advance for students to examine with a microscope. Sample time-lapse videos of fast and slow evaporation are included on this book's companion CD.

Capturing Crystal Formations

- Students should have a few minutes to practice using the time-lapse photography feature on the digital microscope or other software they will be using before beginning this activity (a wristwatch with a moving second hand is good for practice).

- The length of time required for slow evaporation will vary depending on the climate of your classroom. Evaporation time will also depend on the size of the water drop. Using a toothpick to spread the water drop on the slide will increase its surface area. Students should try to prepare both slides the same way.

- A small piece of dark colored construction paper under the slide will increase contrast and make the crystals more visible.

- Several minutes may pass before crystal formation is visible, especially for the cold water drop. If students are available to watch the drops closely, they may want to wait to begin the time-lapse photography until they can see crystals beginning to form. This will avoid the creation of a time-lapse video with a long initial section in which nothing appears to be happening.

Science in Old Maps
Earth Science
GRADE LEVELS: 5–8

Objectives

- Students will identify streams and rivers on a county map.

- Students will determine the number and locations of the resulting watersheds.

NETS•S Addressed

1. Basic operations and concepts

- Students demonstrate a sound understanding of the nature and operation of technology systems.

- Students are proficient in the use of technology.

3. Technology productivity tools

- Students use technology tools to enhance learning, increase productivity, and promote creativity.

- Students use productivity tools to collaborate in constructing technology-enhanced models, preparing publications, and producing other creative works.

5. Technology research tools

- Students use technology tools to process data and report results.

6. Technology problem-solving and decision-making tools

- Students use technology resources for solving problems and making informed decisions.

National Science Education Standards Addressed

- Content Standard A (5–8): All students should develop abilities necessary to do scientific inquiry.

- Content Standard D (5–8): All students should develop an understanding of the structure of the Earth system.

Materials Needed

county map from an atlas

high-resolution digital camera and tripod

graphics software that allows for drawing in layers

Web Resources

Chesapeake Bay and Mid-Atlantic from Space
http://chesapeake.towson.edu/landscape/impervious/all_watersheds.asp
   A good Web site that describes watersheds and defines stream order, subwatersheds, and watershed order.

EPA, Surf Your Watershed
http://cfpub.epa.gov/surf/locate/map2.cfm
An interactive Web site that allows users to find major watersheds in the United States.

Activities

MAPS HAVE been an aid to teaching science since the birth of the public school system in the United States. The U.S. Geological Survey has been producing map products for about a century. Before that time, plat maps could be found in local county history books and in the county recorder's office. In preparing for the U.S. centennial celebration in 1876, many counties of older states prepared atlas maps displaying detailed land plots for each township in the county. These maps included primitive roads, railroads, waterways, towns, and locations of individual farmhouses and schools.

ACQUIRE

Many old atlases measured 15 inches by 17 inches, which allowed for more detailed maps. Scanning these maps into a computer for further analysis is difficult because of their large size. However, capturing images of these maps with a digital camera is much easier. Figure 8 is an example of a digitized map of Logan County, Ohio.

ANALYZE

Although the map is quite detailed, it is difficult to see the details on a standard printed page. However, using image editing software, the image can be expanded to larger sizes, and the details can be studied. Some image editors (such as Adobe Photoshop Elements) allow users to create layers on top of the original background image, enabling students to trace specific features of the map. You can eliminate the noncritical map features by creating a layer for the township lines and another layer for the waterways by tracing over these features from the original map layer. In this way, a GIS-like image can be produced, where specific features can be turned on and off just by clicking on a layer. Figure 9 shows an example of three additional layers: county lines, waterways, and a white layer. The white layer serves to mask the original map from which the tracings were made.

> ### PHOTOGRAPHING THE MAP
>
> Take a picture of the map while it lies on a well-lit surface using the camera's highest resolution setting and with the flash off.

What science can be explored with a map such as this? A modern map of the county can be digitized, resized, rotated if needed, and added to the image as another layer. The modern map layer can then be changed to have a certain level of transparency so students can easily compare early and modern waterways.

Do all the waterways shown on the 1875 map belong to the same watershed (a ridge or other landform that separates drainage areas)? This question could be posed to students

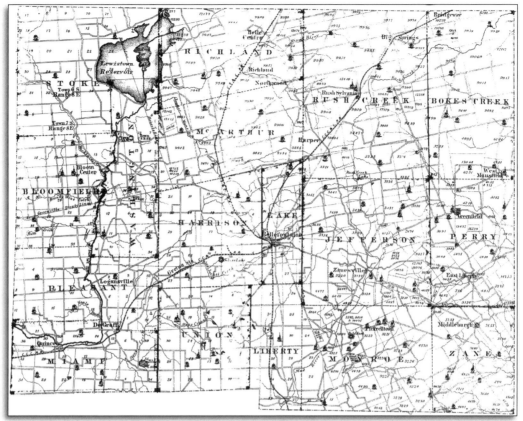

From Combination Atlas Map of Logan County, Ohio, *D. J. Stewart, Philadelphia, Pennsylvania, 1875. Photo by John C. Park.*

FIGURE 8. A detailed map of Logan County, Ohio, from 1875.

while you project the image on the whiteboard. Students should use the projected image as a reference to draw lines on the board to show the watershed boundaries. Another way to explore the watersheds is to put the images on computers so students can create another layer (using the image editing software) on which they draw and shade in their predicted boundaries for each watershed (see Figure 10).

It is difficult to correctly predict all the watersheds, since only Logan County is shown. Some of the waterways might connect into the same system in adjacent counties. To check a broader area, students could use the Internet to obtain additional data.

The teacher can continue to probe with additional questions. Do all the watersheds flow in the same direction? The highest elevation in Ohio is found in Logan County. Where is the probable location of that point based on the waterways shown on the 1875 map? Look for an intersection of three watersheds where one flows west, another flows north, and a third flows south.

Does the highest point in a state indicate a watershed? More information would be needed to answer this question. A map of the rivers in Ohio and the location of Logan County in Ohio would show that all these watersheds flow into two major rivers: the Great Miami

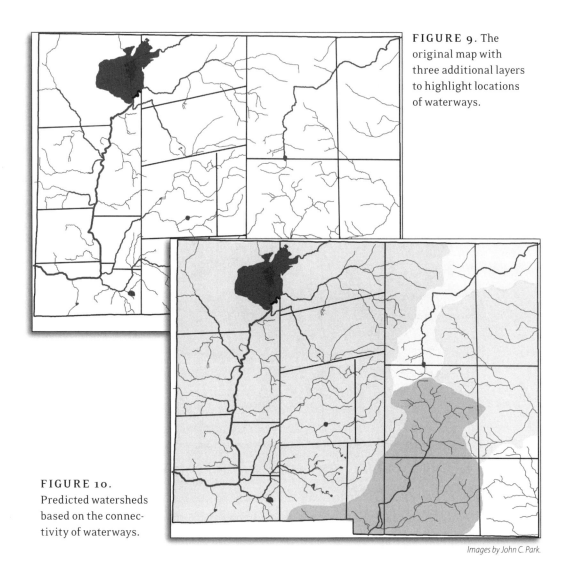

FIGURE 9. The original map with three additional layers to highlight locations of waterways.

FIGURE 10. Predicted watersheds based on the connectivity of waterways.

Images by John C. Park.

River and the Scioto River, both of which flow into the Ohio River. The study of maps can lead to a more integrated approach to science education by including social studies, history, and geography.

CREATE AND COMMUNICATE

Project the map on a whiteboard, and assign each student a home location along a major river on the map. Select a location on a minor tributary of that major river where there will be an environmental spill. Which of the homeowners on the major river will be affected? To what extent will they be affected? Create a new layer on the map that will show where this spill will travel and show the levels of concentration by coloring the lines. Create a flyer that includes this new map warning the homeowners of who is at risk and why.

Predicting Floodplains Using Topographic Maps

Earth Science

GRADE LEVELS: 6–8

Objectives

■ Students will locate areas of flooding using a map with elevation contour lines.

■ Students will predict the consequences of such flooding.

NETS•S Addressed

1. Basic operations and concepts

   • Students demonstrate a sound understanding of the nature and operation of technology systems.

   • Students are proficient in the use of technology.

3. Technology productivity tools

   • Students use technology tools to enhance learning, increase productivity, and promote creativity.

   • Students use productivity tools to collaborate in constructing technology-enhanced models, preparing publications, and producing other creative works.

5. Technology research tools

   • Students use technology tools to process data and report results.

6. Technology problem-solving and decision-making tools

   • Students use technology resources for solving problems and making informed decisions.

National Science Education Standards Addressed

■ Content Standard A (5–8): All students should develop abilities necessary to do scientific inquiry.

■ Content Standard D (5–8): All students should develop an understanding of the structure of the Earth system.

Materials Needed

USGS topographic map

high-resolution camera or scanner

graphics software that allows for drawing in layers

Web Resources

Fear and Flooding in North Carolina
www.southernstudies.org/reports/Princeville-WEB.htm
    Provides information about the flood disaster in Princeville, North Carolina, during Hurricane Floyd.

TopoZone
http://topozone.com
A repository of topographic maps.

Activities

TOPOGRAPHIC MAPS can be used to determine the elevation of locations in an area through the use of contour lines, or lines of equal elevation. In addition to elevation, topographic maps provide other information, such as boundaries, land surface features, water features, building locations, roads, and railroads. A single quadrangle map covers a fairly large area: 7.5 minutes latitude and longitude. Students tend to use only a part of the quadrangle map because of the large amount of information that can be contained by a single map.

ACQUIRE

The United States Geological Survey (USGS) has produced many kinds of maps for all areas in the U.S. The USGS offers topographic maps as 22″ by 24″ paper maps, or as Digital Raster Graphics (DRG) that can be purchased on CD. These topographic maps can also be accessed on the Internet from map download sites, such as TopoZone (**http:// topozone.com**). Since a single quadrangle map contains a lot of information, it is best to select the area of most interest for your students to study. Once obtained, the paper maps can be digitized quickly using a digital camera or scanner.

For purposes of illustration, a map of coastal North Carolina will be used in the description of this activity. In September 1999, the North Carolina coastal plain was devastated by the surge of water produced by Hurricane Floyd. Using a selected area from a standard topographic map, students can map out predicted flood lines for any given elevation.

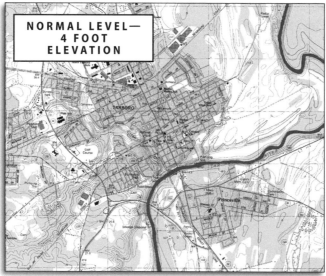

FIGURE 11. This digitized topographic map was made with a layer-capable graphics program. This is the normal level of the Tar River (4 foot elevation).

Image edited by John C. Park.

Images edited by John C. Park.

FIGURE 12. Predicted flood stages of the Tar River using a digitized topographic map and a layer-capable graphics program.

Figures 11 and 12 show a section of a quadrangle map of the Tar River separating Tarboro and Princeville, North Carolina.

ANALYZE

Using the map as a background, students can use software to trace the equal lines of elevation on new layers, each layer signifying a specific elevation. The area bounded by each contour line can be filled with a specific color, and the predicted flood areas may then be viewed.

By examining the detailed features on the map using a computer, students can create hypotheses about the projected flooding problems for a given flood stage. For example, what problems would be created when water treatment plants, cemeteries, or animal waste lagoons are flooded, and at what flood stages might these problems occur for a given location? In this example, major problems begin to occur when the river rises just a few feet above normal level. Princeville is covered at a flood elevation of only 14 feet. Graphics programs can help students identify the potential problem situations when the layers are made visible and invisible by a click of a button.

CONTOUR TIP

In order to fill each contour interval, the contour lines must enclose the area. Be sure to connect the contour lines at the edge of the maps.

CREATE AND COMMUNICATE

Let your students view a topographic map of your area. Are there any locations that could be susceptible to flooding? Remember that there can be flooding in mountains during thunderstorms; flooding does not have to occur at low elevations. When possible areas are located, send a team armed with digital cameras to visit the location. Prepare a document that includes the images that were captured and that area of the topographic map, and send a query to the local officials to see if they can tell you if the area is in a flood zone.

Measuring the Moon
Space Science
GRADE LEVELS: 6–8

Objective

■ Students will measure the relative size of the Moon by measuring photographs captured during a lunar eclipse.

NETS·S Addressed

1. Basic operations and concepts

- Students demonstrate a sound understanding of the nature and operation of technology systems.

- Students are proficient in the use of technology.

5. Technology research tools

- Students use technology tools to process data and report results.

6. Technology problem-solving and decision-making tools

- Students use technology resources for solving problems and making informed decisions.

National Science Education Standards Addressed

■ Content Standard A (5–8): All students should develop abilities necessary to do scientific inquiry.

■ Content Standard D (5–8): All students should develop an understanding of Earth in the solar system.

Materials Needed

video camera and tripod

software to extract images from video, such as iMovie

Geometer's Sketchpad software

Web Resource

Lunar Eclipses for Beginners
www.mreclipse.com/Special/LEprimer.html
 Fred Espenak, Mr. Eclipse, presents one of his many informative Web sites on eclipses. This site describes lunar eclipses and includes a table listing future lunar eclipses.

Activities

MEASUREMENTS CAN be made on still images. Knowing the size of an object in an image can help determine the size of another object beside it using proportions. If the size of an object is not known, then relative measurements can be made. The Geometer's

Sketchpad is a software program that allows students to create analytical geometric sketches. When an image is cut and pasted into the Sketchpad work area, the software provides the necessary tools to make many kinds of measurements.

ACQUIRE

The images displayed in Figure 13 were originally captured on videotape. This was during a lunar eclipse in January 2000, as viewed from Raleigh, North Carolina. The figure demonstrates the use of a manual exposure setting on the camera. All three images were captured within seconds of each other.

> ### MOON SHOT
>
> A camera with a good telephoto zoom is necessary for capturing images of the Moon.

The lower exposure setting for the image on the left allows the viewer to observe the appearance of the Moon's surface. By manually adjusting the exposure, a more defined shadow of the Earth can be seen, as shown in the center image. Further adjustments will provide a clear boundary suitable for measurement, as shown on the right image.

These images were captured using a digital camcorder and videotape. The digital images from the tape were downloaded into software specifically used to edit movies—in this case, iMovie. Specific frames were selected and saved as individual JPEG images and were later merged into one image. Because the image was captured on videotape, it displays some of the characteristics of a single video frame, such as interlacing (incomplete scan lines). Using a progressive scan video camera can solve this problem, or a sequence of images can be captured using a digital still camera.

ANALYZE

Figure 14 shows two screenshots of a Geometer's Sketchpad drawing used to measure the relative size of the Moon compared with the size of the Earth's shadow on the Moon. The image was initially opened using image editing software. The entire image was

Photographs by John C. Park.

FIGURE 13. Captured images of the eclipse of the Moon using various exposure settings.

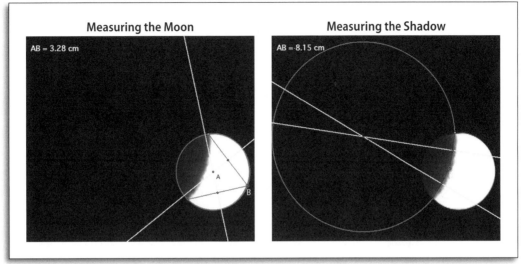

Measuring the Moon

AB = 3.28 cm

Measuring the Shadow

AB = 8.15 cm

Images by John C. Park.

FIGURE 14. The Geometer's Sketchpad was used to measure the relative radii of the Moon and of the Earth's shadow during a lunar eclipse.

selected, cut, and pasted into the Sketchpad workspace. Three points were placed on the edge of the Moon, and two segments were constructed, creating two chords with a common point. Perpendicular bisectors of each chord were constructed, and a point was created at the intersection of the two bisectors. This point represents the center of a circle as determined by the original three points on the Moon's edge. The resulting circle was constructed and the radius of that circle was measured.

The three points set on the Moon's edge produce a circle with a radius measurement of 3.28 cm. When the three points are set at the edge of the Earth's shadow on the Moon, the resulting shadow radius has a measurement of 8.15 cm. The actual radius of the Earth's shadow on the Moon is approximately equal to the radius of the Earth. Knowing this information and the actual radius of the Earth, the Moon's radius can be approximated. This can be done with a ratio: the measured shadow radius is to the measured Moon radius as the actual Earth radius is to the actual Moon radius. Expressed mathematically,

$$\frac{\text{Measured shadow radius}}{\text{Measured Moon radius}} = \frac{\text{Actual Earth radius}}{\text{Actual Moon radius}}$$

$$\frac{8.15 \text{ cm}}{3.28 \text{ cm}} = \frac{6,378 \text{ km}}{x \text{ km}}$$

$$(3.28 \text{ cm} * 6,378 \text{ km}) \quad / \quad 8.15 \text{ cm} = 2,570 \text{ km}$$

In this case, the estimate of the resulting Moon radius is larger than the accepted value of 1,738 km, which is due to the apparent enlargement of the Moon when the camera's light intensity level is increased to get the well-defined shadow line. However, this approximation method results in a good rough estimate of the radius of the Moon.

Investigating a Solar Eclipse
Space Science
GRADE LEVELS: 5–8

Objective

■ Students will discover the motion of the Moon relative to the apparent motion of the Sun.

NETS·S Addressed

5. Technology research tools

- Students use technology tools to process data and report results.

6. Technology problem-solving and decision-making tools

- Students use technology resources for solving problems and making informed decisions.

National Science Education Standards Addressed

■ Content Standard A (5–8): All students should develop abilities necessary to do scientific inquiry.

■ Content Standard D (5–8): All students should develop an understanding of Earth in the solar system.

Materials Needed

aluminized Mylar

video camera with tripod

software to extract images from video, such as iMovie

image editing software

slideshow software such as PowerPoint (optional)

Web Resources

BBC: Science and Nature, Space
www.bbc.co.uk/science/space/solarsystem/sun/eclipsecalendar.shtml
   Along with information about solar eclipses, this site displays much information about our solar system.

Future Total Solar Eclipses
www.earthview.com/timetable/futureTSE.htm
   Shows a timetable of total solar eclipses from 1997 to 2035.

NASA Goddard Eclipse Home Page
http://sunearth.gsfc.nasa.gov/eclipse/eclipse.html
   This is a portal page that describes various types of eclipses and transits, and provides links specifically to those topics.

The Science Junction: Solar Eclipse '98
www.ncsu.edu/sciencejunction/depot/simulate/eclipse98/visualize.html
   This Web site simulates the 1998 solar eclipse as seen from any two places on Earth from which it was visible. Users can compare the time and position of the eclipse.

Activities

A SOLAR eclipse occurs when the Moon lines up between the Sun and the Earth. This blocks the Sun for observers on the Earth who are in the Moon's shadow. The relative motions of the Earth and the Moon can be studied using images taken during an eclipse.

ACQUIRE

There are several ways to collect digital images of a solar eclipse, but if you want to capture the image by pointing your digital video camera directly at the Sun, you will need a strong filter. Aluminized Mylar is the recommended filter for this situation. The only light that will get through this filter is the light directly from the Sun. **WARNING: Do *not* look at the Sun through your camera if the eyepiece is not filtered with Mylar.** A video camera is recommended to capture the images on videotape, so you can play it back and select which frames you want to extract from the tape.

Put the camera on a tripod facing south. Pitch the camera's lens toward the sky until the rotation axis of the camera points to the North Star (if your latitude is 36 degrees, you will pitch your camera lens up 54 degrees). Rotate the camera as the Sun moves across the sky. Frame the Sun to be on the left side of the screen and let the rotation of the Earth show the

TRY A TRIPOD

It is best to use a tripod head that can tilt in three dimensions.

apparent motion of the Sun across the screen. You will have to rotate the camera every few minutes to keep the Sun in the frame of view. Be sure to have plenty of tapes available, since a solar eclipse can last for a few hours from start to finish. Feel free to put the time in the display, if desired.

ANALYZE

Watching the unedited videotape would be as much fun as watching paint dry. Instead, the teacher should select specific frames from the videotape to capture and use. For example, you might choose one frame every three minutes. The advantage of having the time showing in the display is that you can easily use the time indicator to select the next frame. The disadvantage is that you might have part of your image obscured by the time display.

The four images in Figure 15 show the annular solar eclipse of 1994 as seen at a roadside rest stop near Monroe, Michigan. The bright area is the Sun, and the Moon is blocking it. Upon inspection, the Sun appears to be moving from the left of the screen to the right of the screen. What is causing that apparent motion? Since the camera was pointed toward the southern sky, left represents east, and right represents west. Does the Moon appear to move at the same rate as the Sun across the sky? In what direction is the Moon traveling with respect to the Sun?

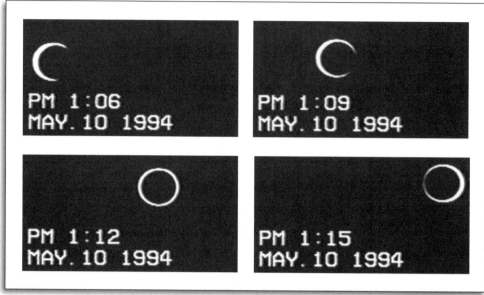

Photographs by Nathaniel Park.

FIGURE 15. Four frames selected from a video of the annular eclipse using a stationary video camera.

CREATE AND COMMUNICATE

There are a number of ways to represent this motion. Using image editing software, the images could be cut and pasted into a single image, showing the progression of the eclipse (Figure 16). One problem with that method is that observers of the image may not know whether the images are progressing from right to left or left to right.

Possibly the most innovative way to present this motion is to create an electronic "flip book" out of the images. Using slideshow software such as PowerPoint, place each image (with the Sun centered on a black background) into a separate slide and set the automatic transition time between slides as short as possible (one second or less is ideal). Another method would be to create a stop-motion animation with the images, as described in the sidebar with the "Metamorphosis of the Butterfly" activity.

Another option is to make an actual flip book. Cut out the printed images (like those in Figure 17), stack them sequentially, and staple the book. Then flip to see the motion of the Moon across the Sun.

Photographs by Nathaniel Park.

FIGURE 16. Four eclipse images at three-minute intervals placed on a single image.

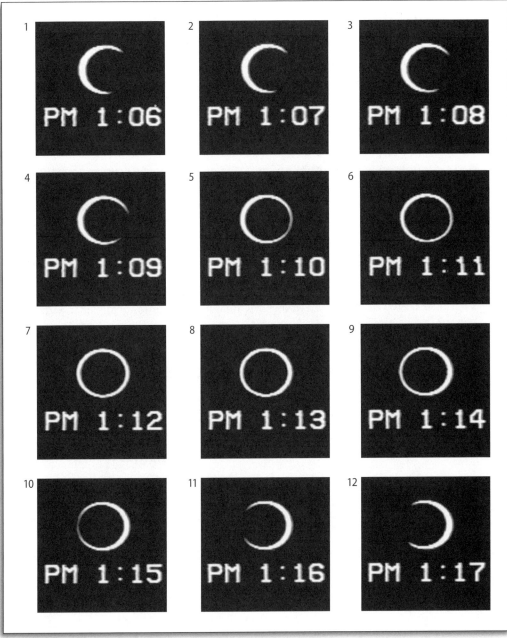

FIGURE 17. Flip book of a solar annular eclipse. Copy page and cut each image with the corresponding number, stack sequentially, and staple.

MODIFICATION

This activity could also be done using time-lapse photography rather than video. A Sun filter would still be needed for the camera lens.

Conclusion

THE ONLY limitations on what can be done using digital imaging tools are the imagination and skill of the science teacher. As a carpenter hones building skills by practicing with various construction tools, a well-versed science educator can help students create solid cognitive structures using the latest imaging tools.

This includes building skills in capturing images using both digital still and digital video equipment. It also includes building skills using image editing software and digital movie software. With imagination, the science teacher and students with basic imaging skills can produce effective environments for science investigation.

DIGITAL IMAGES

The digital images in Figure 17 are available on the CD-ROM accompanying this book.

Resources for More Information

Bowen, A., & Bell, R. L. (2004). Winging it: Using digital imaging to investigate butterfly metamorphosis. *Learning and Leading with Technology, 31*(6), 24-27.

National Research Council. (1996). *National science education standards.* Washington, DC: National Academy Press.

CHAPTER 7

Sara B. Kajder

digital images
in the **language arts** classroom

DAHABO WAS one of 31 seventh graders enrolled in my first period, on-level English class. These seventh graders read and wrote at a variety of levels, mirroring the range of their attention spans, investment in class goals, and curiosity as learners. The learning environment in the classroom changed from day to day, depending on who showed up, what task we were exploring, and how willing the class was to give it a shot. Dahabo quickly blended into the middle of the third row, quietly observing the class and contributing only when prompted, often leading me to question at the close of a busy day if she'd even been present.

SARA B. KAJDER
would like to thank
Janet Swenson for her
invaluable contribu-
tions to this chapter.

Our first novel was Steinbeck's *Of Mice and Men.* Students were happy to view the film version, but initially made minimal progress when it came to engaging with the novel. With much prompting, most students used the stacks of sticky notes made available to them to mark up the novel with ideas and questions. We used these notes to run "hot seat" discussions, enact scenes, construct character journals, and fuel further reading. Momentum built slowly, but as the class became increasingly confident and more engaged, students were increasingly drawn to the text. Dahabo, however, would sit in her group, book in hand, silent. While other student copies of the novel grew fat with colored notes and other signs of active meaning-making, Dahabo's remained slim and closed.

During our weekly reader's conference, Dahabo initially explained her reticence by declaring that, though she understood the models and instructions offered in class, she "didn't have anything to say" about the pages she had read. The more I pushed her, however, the more she revealed. She told me that writing in response to the novel felt awkward because "my words aren't published … they can't live on the same page and mean anything."

It turned out that Dahabo's lack of entries had little to do with her comprehension or understanding of the text and everything to do with her lack of confidence in her role and voice as a reader. As I turned the pages of her reader's log, I noticed that most of her responses were graphic: she depicted her understanding of the text primarily through sketches and drawings. She explained, "I see things in pictures, and I like to write that way."

It was Dahabo's idea to try to use pictures as a means of annotating and marking her way through the novel. She saw it as a way to use her visual skills to represent her understanding, but I saw it as an opportunity for her to have a presence in the text—a visual record of her active construction of meaning. She identified a series of "logographic cues" that would signal different responses to the text (i.e., a chain link fence for an area where a theme or character connected to another text she had read, or a question mark for those areas that generated confusion). Although she initially drew the images onto sticky notes, she later printed digital images onto stickers or added them to her response journal entries for additional reflection and writing. Her library eventually expanded to include 35 different images.

It was the use of visual images that allowed her to enter into a dialogue with the printed text, build on past knowledge, and develop interpretations she felt confident enough of to share with other students. Here, my role as teacher wasn't to equip her with a set of canned annotations (the *what* of marking up a text), but to lead her to see *how* to use her visual mode of understanding to interact with the text. Like Dahabo, students who are encouraged to use their visual intelligence when engaging with literary texts become invested in generating representations and meaning, communicating that understanding to others, and returning to the text to verify, explore, and know.

How Images Can Help Students Learn Language Arts

IMAGES PROVIDE ways for student readers and writers to engage with both visual and printed texts. Digital images offer the added benefit of providing immediacy, accessibility, and even a compelling "hook" into a learning task. Armed with a digital camera, students can capture what they see, often acquiring large libraries of images that are then filtered and narrowed as they work to refine their thinking and meet the specific requirements of the task at hand. Digital images provide an editable text, allowing students to revise image content or combine multiple images into one picture using image editing software. What follows is a general (and certainly not exhaustive) list of possible uses and applications for digital images in the language arts classroom.

DIGITAL IMAGES CAN HELP READERS ENVISION TEXT

Good readers often visualize the action of a story, creating a mental movie of images evoked by the text. Struggling readers often lack this skill. Teachers have sought to address this issue by developing a technique called a *visual think aloud*, which takes a standard classroom reading strategy and transforms it by using video editing tools to develop image sequences organized along digital timelines.

In a traditional *think aloud*, students read printed text orally. They pause to insert their questions, connections, applied reading strategies, and observations. In a *visual think aloud*, students pause to select pictures that represent the mental images the printed text has evoked, and use image editing software to arrange the images and illustrate the story they are reading.

The reading process is usually invisible. Working with a visual think aloud, however, can make steps in that process visible. Images are paired with the text that evokes them and arranged in a narrative sequence. Student readers typically demonstrate a tremendous increase in comprehension when using this strategy. The visual think aloud helps readers work with rich literary texts, developing their understanding through supported visualization. We will say more about how to create and use visual think alouds later in this chapter.

DIGITAL IMAGES OFFER A UNIQUE BRIDGE TO WRITING

Just as digital images provide an entry point for readers, they can also provide an entry point for writers in creating their own texts, whether narrative, persuasive, or expository.

Filmmaker Ken Burns popularized the technique of combining still images with short video clips and a narrated voice-over to create documentaries that bring history to life. Joe Lambert has since developed a variant of that technique at the Center for Digital Storytelling in Berkeley, California (Lambert, 2002). The method he developed with the Center's co-founder, Dana Atchley, allows everyday citizens to create similar documentaries of their own lives. These short digital stories can be used to illustrate a key experience or a new understanding in three minutes or less.

The emerging art of digital storytelling allows students to combine digital images with oral narration to tell their own stories. Effective expression in this medium can be used as a bridge to writing. In some cases, the written script may precede the oral narrative, while in other instances the oral expression may be translated into written form.

DIGITAL IMAGES ALLOW STUDENTS TO COMMUNICATE MEANING VISUALLY

In the two previous applications, digital images serve as scaffolding to make reading and writing more accessible to students. However, there is ample justification for working in this visual medium in its own right. Ultimately, English class is not about printed characters on a sheet of paper, but about communication.

Until now, still and moving images have constituted a "read-only" medium. Digital image editing tools now allow students to write in this format, as well. The emergence of image editing software has made it possible to incorporate new and powerful communication tools into our language arts classes. For example, students have used editing tools such as Adobe Photoshop Elements to create photo collages representing their understanding of a printed text. In secondary classrooms, these have evolved into "open minds": photo collages that graphically represent a character's thoughts at a given point in the text.

> ## CONTENT STANDARDS
>
> The English Language Arts Standards are sponsored by the National Council of Teachers of English and the International Reading Association, www.ncte.org/about/over/standards/.

Teachers can take advantage of the unique capacity of these software tools by fusing image and word. The content created communicates at multiple levels, engaging students on the same terms as media experienced outside the classroom.

POTENTIAL INSTRUCTIONAL USES

The rest of this chapter summarizes potential instructional uses of digital images in the language arts classroom. Anchored to specific, authentic reading and writing tasks, these activities can be directly and effectively mapped to state and national language arts standards. Each includes one or more stages of the acquire-analyze-create-communicate model. Further, each is reflective of promising practices in reading and writing instruction. Digital imaging technology can add to the efficacy of those practices by increasing the level of student engagement and giving students the opportunity to work with multiple forms of text. Digital images can help struggling readers enter texts in compelling, rich ways and allow them to insert their voices into the classroom conversation.

Visual Read Alouds

GRADE LEVELS: 6–8

Objectives

- Students will be able to discuss and analyze their understanding of a select reading passage.

- Students will be able to develop, describe, and evaluate the "mental movie" (or visualization) created when reading print text.

- Students will be able to identify and evaluate the "recitation voice" and "conversation voice" created when reading print text.

NETS•S Addressed

4. Technology communications tools

- Students use a variety of media and formats to communicate information and ideas effectively to multiple audiences.

English Language Arts Standards Addressed

Standard 3—Evaluation Strategies

- Students apply a wide range of strategies to comprehend, interpret, evaluate, and appreciate texts. They draw on their prior experience, their interactions with other readers and writers, their knowledge of word meaning and of other texts, their word identification strategies, and their understanding of textual features (e.g., sound-letter correspondence, sentence structure, context, graphics).

Materials Needed

class texts (i.e., novels, poetry, short stories, nonfiction)

art supplies

databases of images

digital camera

digital video editor (such as iMovie, Movie Maker, or PowerPoint)

QuickTime or Windows Media Player

Literature Resources

Allington, R. L. (2001). *What really matters for struggling readers: Designing research-based interventions.* New York: Longman.

Langer, J. (1995). *Envisioning literature: Literary understanding and literature instruction.* New York: Teachers College.

Activities

READING ALOUD in the classroom is an effective strategy for improving comprehension, whether a teacher is working with low-level elementary students or highly advanced eighth graders. Literature is an invitation to experience, to question, to converse with others, and to see through eyes that aren't our own. Reading literature aloud allows students not only to immerse themselves in the story but also to practice, apply, and later reflect on specific reading strategies. Engaged reading is a visual experience, the text evoking an imagined story world often referred to as a "mental movie." Not only do student readers need to learn how to develop these "mental movies," they also need to be encouraged to explain, connect, and reflect on their own understanding. Students must learn to construct and communicate meaning to others, and reading aloud can help.

Readers construct meaning as they engage with the words on the page. During this stage of the reading process, students should be challenged to figure out how they are making sense of the text through their active, recursive work as readers. Here, instructional goals should include:

- envisioning the textual world

- making and testing predictions

- monitoring understanding

- asking questions

- making connections

By providing adequate scaffolding for these strategies, teachers can help students enter rich literary texts, monitor their thinking, bring ideas into discussion, and apply what they read to their own lives.

In a visual read aloud activity, students read the text, generate visual representations of the story world, and use multimedia presentation or digital video software to fuse the visual elements with a recorded narration of the text. Here, digital imaging technology allows students to create a film-like product that replicates both the visual and oral components of their "mental movie." What makes this activity different from round robin reading paired with a picture is that the reading is conducted and narrated by each student, represented through multiple and varying depictions, and analyzed and discussed by the entire class.

The visual read aloud strategy builds from Langer's (1995, p. 9) notion of "envisionment," in that student representations of the story world are "dynamic sets of related ideas, images, questions, disagreements, anticipations, arguments, and hunches that fill the mind during reading, writing, speaking, or other experiences where one gains, expresses, and shares thoughts and understandings." Through the visual read aloud, students construct a tangible representation of what they see, hear, think, and envision about the text.

Several steps are involved in constructing the visual read aloud, each of which is described below. These steps are illustrated further in the sidebar using Dahabo's experience in developing her work.

ACQUIRE

Students start this activity by first reading the printed text. To help students use these words to envision their own "mental movie," start with a storyboard. Ask students to draw pictures (or select photos) evoked by the story, and sequence these images on paper alongside the appropriate text. Students should be encouraged to represent their ideas graphically by drawing, painting, creating collages (using Photoshop Elements or cutting and pasting images together), or finding or taking photos that express or represent a key element of the story. This planning stage allows students to organize their thoughts and continually revisit the text prior to sitting down at the computer to create their visual read aloud. Depending on the length of the passage, the length of your class period, and any other tasks that students might also be completing, this step can take anywhere from several minutes to two class periods.

Using either a digital camera or a collection of art supplies, the students' next step is to create the visual elements they wish to pair with their narration. Whether they are importing images from the Internet or a compact flash card, or scanning their original art to create a JPEG file, students will need somewhere to store their work—either a portable USB disk drive or a school-provided server account folder that can be accessed from any networked computer. You might require that students take their photos or create their art outside the classroom to maximize their in-school computer time by focusing on importing images and working with the digital video tools.

CREATE

A multimedia presentation tool such as iMovie, Movie Maker, or PowerPoint should be used to import and organize the images, record narration, and add transitions and effects. Students must import the images into the timeline of the digital video tool, a step that should take mere seconds if they have already scanned and saved their images and have them stored in one location. Again, the storyboard can come in handy, as it helps students to sequence all the different materials.

Students should then record their own narration of the passage from the text. It is recommended that these files be recorded one sentence at a time, easing editing and revision. Digital video editors such as iMovie and Movie Maker allow students to record audio and place the resulting files directly into the timeline. Keeping the passage to be read short limits the amount of time that students will need to spend on this step. A shorter passage can also more easily be reentered by students, perhaps in response to further exploration of the meaning.

The final step is for students to sequence the images alongside the narrated clips to ensure that the right words are heard when a particular image appears on the screen. Again, having a manageable passage length helps prevent students from getting overwhelmed and bogged down. Some students might wish to add special effects such as fades, wipes, and other transitions. This should be done in moderation, only when time permits, and (most important), only when it helps to enrich and extend the meaning being conveyed. The last step is to "render" the movie, creating a small QuickTime or Windows Media Player file by exporting the content in the timeline.

ANALYZE

One thing that typically happens when students create visual read alouds is a tremendous growth in their awareness of narrative voice. Many struggling student readers do not hear a narrative voice as their eyes read over the words on the printed page. By joining visual images to an audio track they have recorded themselves, students become sensitized to narrative rhythms and patterns, helping them to hear that voice in later interactions with printed texts. The technology allows students to hear themselves read aloud, creating an artifact they can return to throughout the class for reflection, analysis, and goal setting.

The voices heard internally (and subsequently recorded externally) become more complex as students become more proficient and texts become more challenging. Tovani (2004) identifies these as the "reciting voice" and the "conversation voice." The reciting voice simply reads the words from the page while the conversation voice interacts with those same words, questioning, probing, and unpacking their hidden meanings. For most students, the reciting voice quickly gives way to the conversation voice once they begin to internalize basic reading strategies.

However, students often have a difficult time focusing that voice on the ideas and issues raised in the text. Instead, the voice follows tangents and unrelated topics. In Dahabo's case, this initially led her to stop reading completely. Her eyes pulled from the page, the book closed, and her work shifted from developing understanding to trying to get back to where she thought she was supposed to be in the task. Interestingly, Dahabo wasn't alone. The visual read aloud activity opened a space for the class to discuss narrative voice as we viewed all the students' "finished" products.

Several students pointed out that an important element was missing when we included only the images and the narrated audio track. As one student explained, "I wanted to include the voice I hear as I read this text because it helps *and* hurts when I'm trying to understand what's happening." When asked to identify those areas where "voice" was a distraction, several students pointed to passages with complex syntax and difficult vocabulary. They read, reread, and probed those sections in order to discern what was happening. This work eventually evolved into a visual think aloud activity (described later in this chapter) as students sought to include their thoughts, questions, and challenges in the visual read aloud they had created.

COMMUNICATE

Student-constructed visual read alouds are designed to convey their individual readings of class texts, but they are also class texts themselves, communicating ideas about what it means to read, how readers engage with complex texts, and how we use images to represent and convey understanding.

Essential to this visual read aloud activity is the notion of community. As Lave and Wenger (1991, p. 65) explain, "Learning … is a process of becoming a member of a sustained community of practice … Developing an identity as a member of the community and becoming knowledgably skillful are part of the same process." The visual read aloud can be structured either as an individual or group activity, but it should always be anchored to a classroom community framework in which students are expected to share their ideas and products with one another. For meaning making to advance beyond the pairing of images and text, it is important that "individuals consider multiple ways of interpreting and view individual selves within the class community as interwoven" (Langer, 1995, p. 4).

The strength of the visual read aloud is that it allows students to read text aloud, create their "envisionment," and fuse the two together in an oral and visual product. Teachers should spend significant class time debriefing after each read aloud is viewed, exploring how the narrated text and the visual representations work to convey meaning. This process gives students "a concrete reference as they ask themselves and others: Why did you do that? What else can you do?" (Wilhelm, 1995, p. 498). Further, the end product allows students to see themselves at work as readers, making a largely invisible process quite tangible (and attainable).

Developing Dahabo's Story

When we began the visual read aloud activity, Dahabo was uncertain how to proceed. She started slowly, working to graphically represent her ideas by drawing, creating collages (using Photoshop Elements or cutting and pasting images together), and painting. She explained in a reader's conference, "Now I can't just talk with the book … there is more on the line because I have to show what I see." While some students struggled with their ability to visually represent their ideas, Dahabo was more concerned with the way that she would be positioned in what she created. She explained, "I'm just now figuring out what I want to question and push as I read … but pairing my pictures with the words shows where I am as a reader with this book. That's risky."

Figure 1 offers 30 seconds of Dahabo's work with *Speak*, her self-selected independent reading novel for the first term of the quarter. The sequence of images runs across the screen as she reads a selection from the text which, as a reader, she found to be problematic:

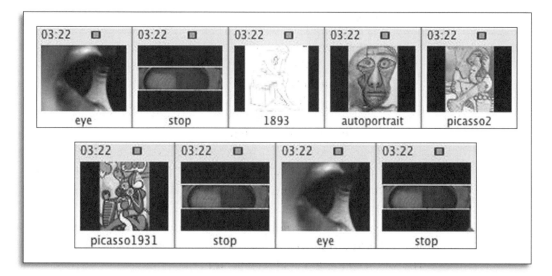

FIGURE 1. Thirty seconds of video sequence from Dahabo's work with the novel *Speak.*

"You need to visit the mind of a Great One," continues Mr. Freeman. Papers flutter as the class sighs. The radio sings louder again. He pushed my pitiful linoleum block aside and gently sits down an enormous book. "Picasso." He whispers like a priest. "Picasso. Who saw the truth. Who painted the truth, molded it, ripped from the earth with two angry hands." He pauses. "But I'm getting carried away." I nod. "See Picasso," he commands, "I can't do everything for you. You must walk alone to find your soul" (Anderson, 2001, p. 118).

The images that she chose were a combination of the logographic cues she'd used to mark the passage and Picasso images that represented her own confusion about what it meant to "see." She explained, "I'm not an artist, but I stopped as soon as I read the last line. I re-read this passage so many times, remembering what I knew about Picasso (which was weirdness—not truth), and thinking about how I see." There was also a connection to Melinda, the novel's protagonist. As Dahabo explained, "The eye is my eye but it's also hers … What pushes me into and out of this book is that I'm often her—and she's often me."

Dahabo emphasized at the close of her first experience in building the visual read aloud that she had a difficult time reaching a stopping point. She offered, "It wasn't that I couldn't pick the passage, it was that the more I worked to show, the more I saw … Reading kept happening."

Logographic Cues

GRADE LEVELS: 5–7

Objectives

- Students will apply their understanding of how readers annotate print text to mark their own paths through select passages.

- Students will use images to represent their responses to print text (such as connections, questions, or areas of confusion).

- Students will discuss and analyze their understanding of select passages of print text.

NETS·S Addressed

3. Technology productivity tools

- Students use technology tools to enhance learning, increase productivity, and promote creativity.

English Language Arts Standards Addressed

Standard 3—Evaluation Strategies

- Students apply a wide range of strategies to comprehend, interpret, evaluate, and appreciate texts. They draw on their prior experience, their interactions with other readers and writers, their knowledge of word meaning and of other texts, their word identification strategies, and their understanding of textual features (e.g., sound-letter correspondence, sentence structure, context, graphics).

Materials Needed

class texts

digital camera

sticker printer paper

Literature Resource

Wilhelm, J. (2004). *Reading is seeing: Learning to visualize scenes, characters, ideas and text worlds to improve comprehension and reflective reading.* New York: Scholastic.

Activities

INSTEAD OF using conventional annotation methods when they read, students can mark up texts using images that represent their responses, ideas, and connections. One of my seventh graders, for example, used a picture of his father's tool bench to indicate those moments in a text where he'd need to "break through" in order to understand what it was expressing. Logographic cues can be printed out as stickers, saved onto the classroom computer for work with electronic text, and added to student response journals for additional reflection and writing. Visual annotation through logographic cues allows student readers to have a presence in the text and encourages active meaning-making as they insert images and responses onto the page.

ACQUIRE AND CREATE

Logographic cues can easily be created in the classroom using a digital camera (or digital image files), a computer, and a printer.

Students first must identify and capture the images to be used. The image needs to be meaningful to the student, calling attention to something specific in the text each time it is used. Students can bring printed images from home that can be scanned or can take their own photos using a digital camera.

Numerous software tools can be used to resize and print images. If you already have a digital camera, chances are students can use the software that came with the camera to open the image file on the computer, select a size, and select the number of prints they would like to make.

Although sticker paper has proven to be most useful for actually annotating the text, students can also transfer the image to a sticky note or simply place it onto a textbook page as a discussion marker. The form the cues need to take to allow your students to use them effectively for annotation will depend on your situation (and your creativity).

ANALYZE AND COMMUNICATE

In this stage, students discuss and evaluate both the images that they use to mark up text and the ways those images allow them to navigate the reading and construct meaning.

The images in Figure 2 are examples of cues that Sam, a sixth grader, captured and saved for use in marking up and annotating texts. Images came from his neighborhood, the school grounds, and an album of his former home in Seattle.

As a reader, Sam would paste these "cues" throughout the text, explaining that he could "put more meaning into a picture than into notes in the margins." Previously, the pages of Sam's textbook were blank, containing no annotations, notes, questions, or reactions. But armed with these logographic cues, Sam quickly became a master annotator. Sam's pages of *The Giver* (Lowry, 2002) were lined with logographic cues and written notes that expanded on what he meant to signal with his cues. In other words, Sam constructed meaning through a process of representation (selecting the image for the cue), identification/connection (locating areas in the text and matching them with logographic cues), communication (placing the image and supplementing with written notes), and interpretation (making meaning by considering the text, the image, and the notes). Sam's metaphor was that the cues functioned as road signs, "showing [him] how to work through the words on the pages."

FIGURE 2. Examples of Sam's visual clues. From top left are "Connections"; "Stop and think. This was difficult."; and "Rich description."

In subsequent work with literary texts, Sam continued to annotate extensively, using a combination of consistent logographic cues and margin notes. These tools provided him with a means to decipher, consider, and connect with the ideas on the printed page. Sam also began participating in class book talks and Socratic seminars, now able to draw on direct textual references drawn from these textual notes.

Vocabulary Pictures

GRADE LEVELS: 4–8

Objective

Students will be able to define vocabulary terms.

NETS•S Addressed

5. Technology research tools

- Students use technology to locate, evaluate, and collect information from a variety of sources.

English Language Arts Standards Addressed

Standard 9—Multicultural Understanding

- Students develop an understanding of and respect for diversity in language use, patterns, and dialects across cultures, ethnic groups, geographic regions, and social roles.

Materials Needed

class vocabulary lists

digital images

printing materials

a tool for organizing images, such as Flikr (**www.flickr.com**)

photo editing software (such as Photoshop Elements or iPhoto)

Activities

FRAN CLAGGETT (1992) described an activity in *Drawing Your Own Conclusions* in which students "draw their vocabulary words." The task challenges students to think carefully about the meaning of the words they are studying, and is designed to improve their understanding and retention. Claggett's strategy can easily be modified for use with digital cameras.

ACQUIRE

Ask students to take photos that represent vocabulary terms they are currently studying. Grade level vocabulary lists tend to be static, lacking a context outside the classroom assignment. Here, students collect images by "reading" their community in an attempt to find "visual definitions" of required vocabulary terms.

The value of this activity can be summarized in these words from a fifth grader: "Taking pictures lets me understand the definition of the word on my own terms. I picture the word, create the picture, and then start to know the word." As opposed to memorizing words on a list, students are actively constructing meaning of terms and connecting it to their lived experiences outside the classroom. Figure 3 shows three examples of a student's "visual vocabulary."

COMMUNICATE

Images can be posted to a class "word wall," which ultimately challenges students to develop a shared visual library.

MODIFICATION

An extension of this activity would be to challenge students to record literacy events experienced outside the classroom. In *Changing Our Minds: Negotiating English and Literacy,* Miles Myers (1996) explains that speech events are an essential part of situated knowledge, offering students opportunities not only to study language in action but also to examine differences between presentational and conversational modes of communication. Extensive discussion in class subsequently explores how students can use images to capture oral texts and bring meaning into being. Building on student visual and verbal literacy skills, these images can be paired with written reflections that explain the event, the meaning it represents, and how it enriches, complicates, or challenges the student's understanding of literacy.

FIGURE 3. Examples of vocabulary pictures. Top left is "Cumulative," bottom left is "Intermittent," and right is "Voice."

Visual Literacy Narratives

GRADE LEVELS: 4–8

Objectives

- Students will use images to communicate intended meaning.
- Students will use their understanding of their experiences and work as readers to have richer, more successful interactions with print text.

NETS·S Addressed

4. Technology communications tools

- Students use a variety of media and formats to communicate information and ideas effectively to multiple audiences.

English Language Arts Standards Addressed

Standard 5—Communication Strategies

- Students employ a wide range of strategies as they write and use different writing process elements appropriately to communicate with different audiences for a variety of purposes.

Materials Needed

digital camera

digital images

multimedia presentation tool or digital video editing software (such as PowerPoint, iMovie, or Adobe Premiere)

Literature Resource

Myers, M. (1996). *Changing our minds: Negotiating English and literacy.* Urbana, IL: National Council of Teachers of English.

Activities

ONE OF the most powerful writing prompts in a language arts classroom is to ask students to write about their own experiences as readers and writers. Literacy narratives invite students' own stories and experiences into the classroom, providing a writing space where students can explore what they know about their own literacy skills and experiences. As Miles Myers points out in *Changing Our Minds* (1996, p. 130), "Reading and writing are acts of self definition," and the literacy narrative is a space for students to explore those selves.

Visual literacy narratives require students to construct a digital story, using PowerPoint slides, iMovie, or Adobe Premiere, to communicate their experiences as readers and writers. For example, Pacey, a seventh grade student, wrote about the school media center and his introduction to reading outside the classroom. Using images of the media center and the stacks of books that he had explored (see Figure 4), this student's visual narrative both showed a reader in action and celebrated the people who had passed a book his way. The narration paired with his original images is included the following passage:

I DON'T HANG OUT IN LIBRARIES. I stopped in the media center because it was the one place that wasn't littered with kids that I didn't know and who didn't seem at all interested in the Navy brat who had just stumbled through the door. The librarian, Mrs. Pearson, noticed me, called me over and handed me a card. I didn't know what to say or think. She thought I was a reader. The card had my name on it, and there was something oddly attractive about how the plastic cover caught the light. She handed me a book and nodded toward the couch in the corner, away from the window. It was as if she knew.

It took me forever to read. I was so slow that I'd forget what was on the top of the page by the time that I'd worked my way down to the bottom. That first book took me over a month to finish, and I can't even tell you its title. What I can tell you is that I kept coming back, and, each time, she handed me a book to get lost in. She wasn't just giving me books. She was giving me a window into a world I'd never known.

Screenshot courtesy of Apple.

FIGURE 4. iMovie timeline segment of a seventh grader's visual literacy narrative.

ACQUIRE AND CREATE

In this activity, students use a variety of original still, moving, and scanned images, which they arrange in a timeline.

Pacey used a digital camera to capture short, 10- to 30-second videos demonstrating the paths he had taken as a reader. When placed alongside still images of books and passages in which he narrated what it meant to think and work as a reader, these videos added up to a powerful, authentic, reflective narrative of where this student was and where he wanted to go next as a reader. Further, it provided us with a "text" of his reading to which we were able to return throughout the semester to track his progress and skill development.

COMMUNICATE

The audience for students' visual literacy narratives is other readers and writers, expanding the class community and offering rich opportunities for authentic response and assessment.

Pacey's visual narrative provided him with a space for self-reflection about his own work as a reader, but also challenged him to communicate those ideas in a way that would be accessible and meaningful to other readers in and beyond the classroom. Pacey's class-room teacher held a public screening of the narratives, inviting teachers, parents, and community members to participate in the audience. Students "opened" each piece with a description of their work and an invitation for feedback from the audience. After each was shared, students debriefed with the audience, establishing connections and building community as readers, and focusing on those areas of the story that were the most powerful or resonant for the viewers.

Visual literacy narratives capture a student's understanding of his or her literacy at a particular moment in time. Consequently, they are perfect artifacts for portfolio reflec-tion and written peer review. Students might also revise their story throughout the semester, reflecting their ongoing growth and experience.

Visual Think Alouds

GRADE LEVELS: 5–8

Objective

- Students will discuss, analyze, and evaluate their comprehension of a select passage by examining their mental movie, readers' voices, and think aloud responses.

NETS•S Addressed

3. Technology productivity tools

- Students use productivity tools to collaborate in constructing technology-enhanced models, preparing publications, and producing other creative works.

English Language Arts Standards Addressed

Standard 3—Evaluation Strategies

- Students apply a wide range of strategies to comprehend, interpret, evaluate, and appreciate texts. They draw on their prior experience, their interactions with other readers and writers, their knowledge of word meaning and of other texts, their word identification strategies, and their understanding of textual features (e.g., sound-letter correspondence, sentence structure, context, graphics).

Materials Needed

digital camera

digital images

class text

digital video editing software such as iMovie or Movie Maker

QuickTime Player or Windows Media Player

concept mapping software such as Inspiration (optional)

Literature Resources

Cunningham, P. M., & Allington, R. (2003). *Classrooms that work: They can ALL read and write* (3rd ed.). Boston: Pearson Education.

Harvey, S., & Goudvis, A. (2000). *Strategies that work: Teaching comprehension to enhance understanding.* Portsmouth, NH: Heinemann.

Activities

IN THE article "Reading Is Seeing," Jeffrey Wilhelm (1995, p. 120) defines the act of reading as the "reader's evocation of the text as imagined, visualized, and experienced." Engaged reading is a visual experience, the text evoking an imagined story world in the mind's eye. Not only do student readers need to learn to develop these "mental movies" from the words on the page, they must also learn to explain, connect, and reflect on the text with their own storytelling, thereby constructing and communicating meaning for others.

The think aloud is a well known and effective research-based practice commonly used in reading instruction. In a think aloud, readers read the text out loud, pausing at intervals to insert their own comments and reflection. This strategy makes the mostly invisible reading process tangible and open to discussion and analysis. Think alouds can be presented either orally or in print; a written think aloud challenges the reader to record responses, thoughts, questions, and ideas next to the text segments that are being addressed. Expert readers use the think aloud as a space for inference, connection, and elaboration, whereas novice readers typically use it as a place to connect details and develop a literal reading. Think alouds can demonstrate and model what good readers do, showing how they apply strategies to envision the text and keep all the information straight.

The visual think aloud reworks this strategy by fusing oral and print texts with digital images, depicting the interpretive work of the reader through the visual imagery elicited by the text.

ACQUIRE AND CREATE

Using digital images and digital video editing software, students create a short digital movie that includes a visual representation of their imagined story world, together with two narrated audio tracks. Students can take their own pictures or scan original or found art. One of the audio tracks should be dedicated to their verbatim reading of the story (the read aloud). The second should be used for inserting their think aloud comments and connections. The finished product fuses the read aloud and think aloud, using digital images and video software to communicate the reader's unique understanding of the literary text. Students use the visual think aloud framework to infer, predict, connect, decode, and converse with the author.

The steps in creating a visual think aloud are similar to those in the "Visual Read Alouds" section in this chapter, except that students are working with two audio tracks, not just one.

Students should start capturing their "conversation" with the print text as soon as they begin reading. Equipped with sticky notes or pads of paper, students should note areas in the text where they see connections with another book or a prior experience, questions that come up as they read, observations about the writer's style, predictions, evaluation comments, or any other "aha" moments.

Next, students should compile their notes and plan a visual component to go along with them. Students can use paper and pencil (or software such as Inspiration) to map each image, technique, and element of their envisioned story world, pulling it all together to construct a storyboard.

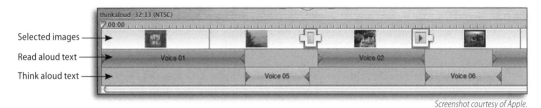

Selected images →

Read aloud text →

Think aloud text →

FIGURE 5. iMovie timeline from a student's visual think aloud.

Students then import their images into the digital video timeline—a step that should take only a few seconds if they have already scanned and saved their images and stored them in one location. The storyboard comes in handy for sequencing the images appropriately.

Students then record their read aloud of the print text. Next, they record their think aloud notes, inserting them into the video's second audio track (see Figure 5). Each audio line will color the track differently (e.g., Track 1 files are purple, and Track 2 files are orange). It is recommended that an additional layer of organization be added to clarify the naming of files: read aloud sentences should include the letters "ra" in the file name, while think aloud sentences should include the letters "ta." For example, the first sentence of a think aloud could be saved as "1_ta," and the second sentence of a read aloud could be saved as "2_ra."

Finally, students sequence the images with the two audio tracks, while possibly adding special effects and transitions to signal those moments when the "viewer" needs to pay particular attention to what is being said. Most students, however, will probably use little more than "fade" or "wipe" transitions and an occasional pan across an image. The final step is to "render" the movie, creating a small QuickTime or Windows Media Player file by exporting the content in the timeline.

COMMUNICATE

Students use the visual think aloud to represent their work as readers when engaging with a printed text. Although the audience is largely themselves, students are also working collaboratively with others in the class literacy community to develop readings, articulate strategies, and represent their processes.

When used in the classroom, the visual think aloud opens a space where individual student voices can be heard. My experience with this strategy has confirmed Kylene Beers' (2002, p. 104) view that "it's more critical for dependent readers to talk about texts during the reading than after it." With a bit of scaffolding, work on a visual think aloud project empowers students to talk about texts before, during, and after their reading. Further, it provides an immediate opportunity for teachers to provide guided practice, discuss student understanding, and assist with higher order thinking skills.

Reading is not just about "decoding" a printed text, it is also a process of encoding it with personal meaning, and the visual think aloud provides a perfect vehicle for doing just that. One student described it best, offering that her work on a visual think aloud project "was the first time that reading actually made sense."

MODIFICATION

One reinvention of the visual think aloud activity just described is to use the second audio track to record a *class* think aloud. Instead of focusing on an individual reading, interrupted reading allows for multiple student voices to enter into conversation with the text, interrupting a read aloud to talk about some aspect of the text. This strategy is very useful for modeling active reading strategies to the full class and can invite reluctant student voices into the larger class discussion. It can also work well with small groups.

No matter how this technique is adapted, the fundamental elements are the same: students create a visual representation of the story world, record themselves reading the story and save this as one audio track, and record a second audio track with responses, questions, comments, and reflections from as many group or class members as possible.

Managing the Technology

FOR ALL OF THESE "DURING READING" activities, it is important to make sure that the technology adds instructional value to the task and doesn't become a distraction. Many of these same tasks can be accomplished using magazines, scissors, and construction paper; however, software tools such as iMovie and Movie Maker allow students to generate short, animated films that more authentically represent the way they see the mental movies evoked by a text.

Yes, learning to use these software tools requires a greater investment of time, but that investment is usually paid back many times in increased understanding and student use of effective comprehension strategies. Many of the activities described in this chapter were student-initiated, building from the unique talents and skills they brought to the classroom. Whenever using new technology in the classroom, teachers should ask themselves the following questions:

■ What is the value added by using technology in this activity?

■ What resources are at my disposal?

■ What do I need to know in order to make this work?

Conclusion

LEARNING ISN'T primarily about absorbing or transmitting knowledge; it's about thinking and providing students with authentic experiences to transform what they know. What my colleagues and I have discovered in the short time we have been working with digital images in the language arts classroom is that effective teaching practices paired with powerful technologies provide student readers and writers with unique experiences that can transform their understanding of texts, words, and images. Literacy demands that students communicate and make meaning from a variety of texts, all of which must be incorporated and understood within the context of their personal lives. All language arts teachers want their students to become lifelong readers, writers, listeners, and thinkers—and perhaps even seers.

Incorporating digital images into the curriculum provides students with new, engaging opportunities to work with and create texts. Reading instruction is about leading students to a more complete and complex understanding of how texts work and what strategies good readers and writers use to unlock their secrets. The activities described in this chapter can add to a student's toolkit of reading strategies and, more important, to the student's modes of entry into rich literary texts. Images allow students to represent what they think they know, connect the new to the known, and express their understanding in ways that are visual, auditory, scholarly, and powerful.

These activities and strategies are, of course, just the beginning of what we anticipate to be a much longer list of practices for leading students visually and verbally into close, mindful interactions with text. They are simultaneously a glimpse of the possibilities and an invitation for teachers to examine, invent, reinvent, and join in the conversation.

Resources for More Information

Anderson, L. (2001). *Speak.* New York: Puffin Press.

Beers, K. (2002). *When kids can't read.* Portsmouth, NH: Heinemann.

Claggett, F. (1992). *Drawing your own conclusions.* Portsmouth, NH: Heinemann.

Daniels, H. (2003, July). *This stupid job!* Keynote delivered at the Walloon Institute, Lake Geneva, WI.

Lambert, J. (2002). *Digital storytelling: Capturing lives, creating community.* Berkeley, CA: Digital Diner.

Langer, J. (1995). *Envisioning literature: Literary understanding and literature instruction.* New York: Teachers College.

Lave, J., & Wenger, E. (1991). *Situated learning: Legitimate peripheral participation.* New York: Cambridge University Press.

Lowry, L. (2002). *The giver.* New York: Laurel Leaf Books.

Myers, M. (1996). *Changing our minds: Negotiating English and literacy.* Urbana, IL: National Council of Teachers of English.

Tovani, C. (2004). *Do I really have to teach reading?* Portland, ME: Stenhouse.

Wilhelm, J. (1995). Reading is seeing: Using visual response to improve the literary reading of reluctant readers. *Journal of Reading Behavior, 27*(4), 467-503.

CHAPTER 8

Brian Sharp, Ann Thompson, and Joe Garofalo

digital images
in the **mathematics** classroom

TEACHERS GENERALLY agree that technology, when used effectively, can promote teaching and learning. Indeed, the Technology Principle of the National Council of Teachers of Mathematics' (NCTM) *Principles and Standards for School Mathematics* (2000, p. 24) states: "Technology is essential in teaching and learning mathematics; it influences the mathematics that is taught and enhances students' learning. Electronic technologies—calculators and computers—are essential tools for teaching, learning, and doing mathematics."

Note

This chapter is an expanded version of Sharp, Garofalo, and Thompson (2004).

The most prevalent technology in mathematics classrooms today is the graphing calculator. This is due to a variety of reasons, including cost, portability, and the calculator's ability to help students connect algebraic, numerical, and graphical representations. Some well-regarded software programs are also widely used in mathematics teaching, such as the Geometer's Sketchpad, an excellent tool for helping students visualize mathematical concepts and relationships.

How Digital Imagery Supports Curricular Goals

THE NCTM Principles and Standards for School Mathematics include numerous references to the importance of visualization and the usefulness of electronic technologies to generate images. Although the focus of the NCTM discussion of technology is on calculators and computers, and the images they refer to are primarily graphs and tables, the argument can certainly be extended to include digital cameras and digital images. Furthermore, the current emphasis on generating multiple representations of mathematics concepts so that students can view them from multiple perspectives can be directly supported through the use of digital images. Digital cameras are inexpensive and portable. They can be used both on their own and in conjunction with graphing calculators and computer programs to supplement standard mathematical representations with real-world images. The emerging field of digital imaging offers new and intriguing possibilities for mathematics educators wishing to create authentic mathematics problems and environments for students.

CONTENT STANDARDS

The Principles and Standards for School Mathematics are sponsored by the National Council of Teachers of Mathematics, http://standards.nctm.org/.

In this chapter, we explore several ways that digital imagery can support sound pedagogical and curricular goals. Many other uses for digital imagery exist, of course, and many more uses will be discovered as digital cameras and Internet access become more ubiquitous in our schools. The examples we present can be grouped into three basic areas:

■ mathematical analyses of digital images

■ digital story problems

■ stories about mathematics in the world

These examples illustrate the acquire-analyze-create-communicate framework presented in chapter 1, as each of these steps in the iterative process plays an important role in the mathematical use of digital images. The *acquiring* step provides students with the opportunity to create and collect digital images that express mathematical concepts in everyday life. When *analyzing* images, students discover the mathematical meaning of the images they have collected. The *creating* step allows students to use mathematical images for focused projects and goals. Finally, *communicating* their work allows students to stimulate conversation and sharing about their work and mathematics in the real world. Throughout the chapter, we will indicate how student and teacher activities exemplify this digital imaging framework.

Mathematically Analyzing Digital Images

ONE MAJOR use of digital images in the mathematics classroom involves the collection and analysis of authentic examples of mathematical patterns and concepts. In most cases, teachers and students will acquire images that illustrate a particular concept and then organize these images for analysis. Using a variety of software tools, learners will then create mathematical analyses of the images and communicate their findings. The first three activities—"Analyzing Slopes of Rooftops," "Finding and Using Vanishing Points," and "Investigating Areas of Irregular Figures"—use the Geometer's Sketchpad to analyze the mathematical aspects of digital images.

Creating Contexts for Story Problems

TRADITIONALLY, MUCH of mathematics has been taught in an isolated and somewhat sterile context. Problem solving has often meant solving word problems that are written to provide practice in particular mathematical skills. Most students of mathematics remember some of the mindless rules taught and used in the solving of unrealistic story problems that involved boats traveling upstream, interest on loans, or numbers of pencils available for classrooms. For many, story problems are associated with confusion and frustration; the idea that a story problem might actually be interesting or motivating is far outside the experience of most mathematics students. Yet story problems remain a significant part of the mathematics curriculum, and the primary way that problem-solving skills are taught and assessed.

Creating authentic and compelling story problems is a significant challenge for the mathematics educator. Success comes from looking for ideas in the events of everyday life and presenting them in context, using the storyteller's art to engage students in rich and meaningful problem-solving. Skilled teachers of mathematics help students to define problems, enjoy problems, and invent solutions to problems, and communicate their own enthusiasm for the process.

The digital camera and the emerging field of digital storytelling offer teachers and students new ways to create and solve authentic, real-world story problems. At the simplest level, teachers can use digital cameras to create story problems out of captured images or events, and then encourage students to create and illustrate their own digital math story problems. Armed with cameras and looking for story material, students will begin to view the world around them as a potential mathematics problem. The statement "math is everywhere" takes on a new meaning for a student with a digital camera looking to create a story problem for peers.

Digital stories can be created from daily events and should emphasize the importance of mathematics in everyday life. A good digital story problem will have an interesting plot and contain both relevant and irrelevant data that students must sort through to come up with the correct solution. Two activities, "Proportional Reasoning" and "Storm of the Century," provide examples of digital story problems.

Digital Stories about Mathematics

IN ADDITION to using digital images to create digital mathematics story problems, students can use digital cameras and images to create stories *about* mathematics in everyday life. Teachers can assign digital story authoring projects for mathematics in general or for particular topics being addressed in their classroom. Topics such as geometry, estimation, or percentage can provide useful frames for student stories. Discovering and describing authentic mathematics situations will help students cross the divide between school mathematics and real-world mathematics.

Involving parents and community members in the creation of these digital stories will provide opportunities for students to discuss mathematics with adults and will also expand the content possibilities for the stories. Jointly creating digital stories about mathematics can be a challenging and rewarding activity for adults and children alike. Simple frames for stories such as "Geometry in Our Neighborhood" can provide the opportunity for children and adults to engage in lively discussions as they create a story around this topic. Suggestions for parent/child digital stories include:

- mathematics in Dad's or Mom's work

- mathematics and our pets

- mathematics and cooking

- mathematics and building

- mathematics in art

- mathematics in nature

- mathematics in the garden

The activity "The Girl Who Loved Math" is an example of one such story.

Analyzing Slopes of Rooftops
Mathematically Analyzing Digital Images
GRADE LEVELS: 7–9

Objective

■ Students will develop and explore the concept of slope in realistic settings.

NETS·S Addressed

1. Basic operations and concepts

   • Students are proficient in the use of technology.

3. Technology productivity tools

   • Students use technology tools to enhance learning, increase productivity, and promote creativity.

4. Technology communications tools

   • Students use a variety of media and formats to communicate information and ideas effectively to multiple audiences.

5. Technology research tools

   • Students use technology to locate, evaluate, and collect information from a variety of sources.

6. Technology problem-solving and decision-making tools

   • Students use technology resources for solving problems and making informed decisions.

Mathematics Standards Addressed

Algebra Standard: Instructional programs from prekindergarten through Grade 12 should enable all students to:

   • Understand patterns, relations, and functions

   • Represent and analyze mathematical situations and structures using algebraic symbols

   • Use mathematical models to represent and understand quantitative relationships

   • Analyze change in various contexts

Connections Standard: Instructional programs from prekindergarten through Grade 12 should enable all students to:

   • Recognize and apply mathematics in contexts outside of mathematics

Materials Needed

digital images of linear phenomena

dynamic geometry software such as the Geometer's Sketchpad

Activities

THE CONCEPT of *slope* is important in mathematics. It is first introduced in pre-algebra courses, but is further developed in algebra, geometry, and calculus. Although slope is used in many applied situations, it is too often introduced in schools in abstract and procedural ways that are disconnected from real-world situations (e.g., $\Delta y/\Delta x$). Use of digital imagery can help students to bridge the gap between the abstract definition of slope and its concrete applications. Pictures of rooftops can provide a real-world context for teaching and exploring slope.

ACQUIRE

Students can acquire a collection of images of a wide variety of rooftops by using a digital camera to take their own pictures or by downloading images from the Internet. This collection should include the roofs of different structures in a variety of geographic locations. For example, the collection could include an A-frame at a ski resort, a north-eastern Cape Cod house, an industrial structure, a school, a ranch-style house, and a southwestern pueblo.

ANALYZE

These images can then be imported into computer programs, such as the Geometer's Sketchpad, for analysis. In Sketchpad, students anchor their pictures onto a scalable coordinate plane and place data points on the roofs near the eave and near the peak. Using Sketchpad features, they can display the coordinates for each point and use them to calculate the slope of the roof, or they can construct a line through the points and display the slope of the line (see Figure 1).

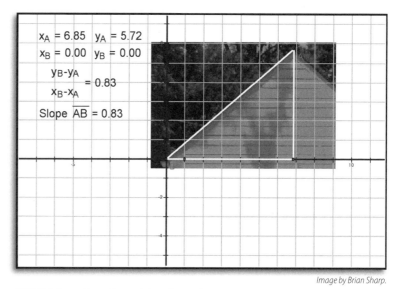

Image by Brian Sharp.

FIGURE 1. A rooftop with a slope of 0.83.

CREATE AND COMMUNICATE

Once students analyze their collection of rooftops, they can create a slideshow showing the rooftops, the respective slopes, and the geographic locations of the structures. Students can use their slideshow to explain how factors such as the environment, building cost, and city codes influence the design of roofs. For example, in areas with large amounts of snowfall, rooflines are often steep so that snow readily slides off. Large commercial structures, such as a Wal-Mart, often use relatively flat roofs because the cost of building a sloped roof over such an expansive building would be too great.

MODIFICATIONS

In addition to the activities described above, students can also manipulate their digital images of houses or buildings to see how they would look with different rooflines. At a more advanced level, students can plot data points and determine mathematical functions that model nonlinear roofs (for example, domes or multi-tiered roofs) to explore connections between roof designs and cultural and environmental influences.

Finding and Using Vanishing Points
Mathematically Analyzing Digital Images
GRADE LEVELS: 5–9

Objective

■ Students will develop and explore the concept of vanishing point.

NETS·S Addressed

1. Basic operations and concepts

- Students are proficient in the use of technology.

3. Technology productivity tools

- Students use technology tools to enhance learning, increase productivity, and promote creativity.

4. Technology communications tools

- Students use a variety of media and formats to communicate information and ideas effectively to multiple audiences.

5. Technology research tools

- Students use technology to locate, evaluate, and collect information from a variety of sources.

6. Technology problem-solving and decision-making tools

- Students use technology resources for solving problems and making informed decisions.

Mathematics Standards Addressed

Geometry Standard: Instructional programs from prekindergarten through Grade 12 should enable all students to:

- Analyze characteristics and properties of two- and three-dimensional geometric shapes and develop mathematical arguments about geometric relationships

- Use visualization, spatial reasoning, and geometric modeling to solve problems

Algebra Standard: Instructional programs from prekindergarten through Grade 12 should enable all students to:

- Use mathematical models to represent and understand quantitative relationships

Materials Needed

digital images of flat and perspective paintings

dynamic geometry software such as the Geometer's Sketchpad

Activities

PRIOR TO the 15th century, most paintings were "flat"; that is, they did not account for perspective. The result was scenes that do not look realistic. For example, notice that in Simone Martini's *The Carrying of the Cross* (1325), the heads of people in the background are not smaller than those of the people in the foreground (see Figure 2).

FIGURE 2. Simone Martini, *The Carrying of the Cross*, 1325, from the Orsini Altarpiece, Louvre, Paris, France.

During the Renaissance, artists began incorporating a sense of perspective into their work. This gave their paintings a more realistic look. One way they incorporated perspective was through the use of a "vanishing point," the point of a painting where parallel lines intersect. Notice in da Vinci's *The Last Supper* (1498) how the use of a vanishing point gives the painting a sense of realism (see Figure 3). In this painting, the parallel lines in the ceiling tiles and along the walls all intersect at a single point on the head of Christ, the focus of the painting.

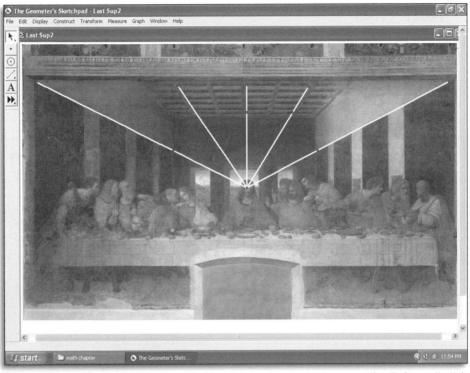

FIGURE 3. Imported into the Geometer's Sketchpad is Leonardo da Vinci's *The Last Supper*, 1498, post-restoration, S. Maria delle Grazie, Milan, Italy.

ACQUIRE AND ANALYZE

Students can acquire digital images of artworks that incorporate vanishing points or use their own digital photographs of scenes that contain parallel elements. As in Figure 3, they can use the Sketchpad to analyze their images by constructing "parallel" lines that identify the location of vanishing points.

CREATE AND COMMUNICATE

After developing an understanding and appreciation of the use of vanishing points, students can design their own templates with parallel lines and vanishing points in order to create perspective drawings. Such experiences with perspective drawings will allow students to communicate the differences between perspective and nonperspective drawings at a much deeper level. It will help them determine the elements of a drawing or painting that the artist wants to feature, and how to use a vanishing point to construct their own perspective drawings.

Investigating Areas of Irregular Figures
Mathematically Analyzing Digital Images
GRADE LEVELS: 4–9

Objective

- Students will develop and explore the concept of area in a realistic setting.

NETS·S Addressed

1. Basic operations and concepts

- Students are proficient in the use of technology.

3. Technology productivity tools

- Students use technology tools to enhance learning, increase productivity, and promote creativity.

4. Technology communications tools

- Students use a variety of media and formats to communicate information and ideas effectively to multiple audiences.

5. Technology research tools

- Students use technology to locate, evaluate, and collect information from a variety of sources.

6. Technology problem-solving and decision-making tools

- Students use technology resources for solving problems and making informed decisions.

Mathematics Standards Addressed

Geometry Standard: Instructional programs from prekindergarten through Grade 12 should enable all students to:

- Analyze characteristics and properties of two- and three-dimensional geometric shapes and develop mathematical arguments about geometric relationships
- Use visualization, spatial reasoning, and geometric modeling to solve problems

Materials Needed

digital images of two- and three-dimensional objects

dynamic geometry software such as the Geometer's Sketchpad

a copy of a Geometer's Sketchpad sketch that contains an adjustable grid (available on the CD accompanying this book).

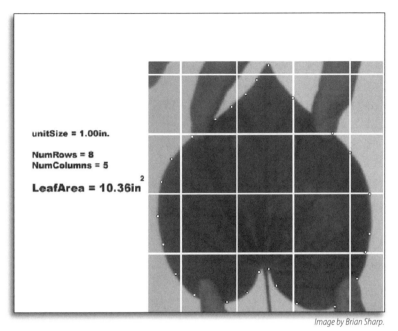

unitSize = 1.00in.

NumRows = 8
NumColumns = 5

LeafArea = 10.36in^2

Image by Brian Sharp.

FIGURE 4. An image of a leaf imported into the Geometer's Sketchpad.

Activities

TO HELP children understand the concepts of *area* and *perimeter*, elementary teachers utilize a variety of strategies. One strategy is to have children piece together Unifix Cubes on their desks. Once figures are constructed, children count the cubes to determine the areas of the figures they have created. A second strategy is to have children find the areas of figures that have been superimposed on a grid of unit squares. Children determine the areas of such figures by counting the squares that are covered by the figures. This process often involves estimation when the outline of a figure does not completely cover a square. Both strategies tend to present area and perimeter in a decontextualized way—or, at best, in a context created by the teacher. Since the concepts of area and perimeter are present in many applied situations, it seems logical that children should create and solve problems that are of interest to them and have a real-world connection. The use of digital imagery can help children bridge the gap between decontextualized problems and concrete applications.

In this activity, children investigate the areas of leaves. However, the activity can be adjusted to accommodate almost any small object that interests children.

ACQUIRE

Students first need to capture digital images of leaves, preferably by using a digital camera. Teachers may choose to have their students investigate images of the same leaf, or let them work on a picture of a leaf of their own choosing. When the children take their pictures, they need to make sure that they hold the camera parallel to the flat surface on which the leaves are placed. They should also be close enough so that their leaves fill as much of their camera's viewing window as possible. In order to accurately measure the area, each picture must also contain an object of known length. This is best accomplished by placing a ruler just below the bottom of each leaf. Once the pictures are downloaded onto a computer, students can use a photo editing program to crop the images and copy them onto their computer's clipboard.

ANALYZE

Students should then paste their pictures into a Geometers' Sketchpad sketch that contains an *adjustable grid*. Students will use this adjustable grid to determine the area of their leaves. A copy of a Geometers' Sketchpad sketch that contains an adjustable grid is included on the CD-ROM accompanying this book (the directions for the remainder of this activity will be based on that sketch).

In Sketchpad, students paste their pictures onto the workspace containing the adjustable grid; both the picture and the grid will remain visible. After pasting their pictures onto the workspace, students will need to adjust the size of the grid to encompass their pictures. This is accomplished by adjusting the number of rows and columns that make up the grid. The default size of each grid square is one unit by one unit. Students will also need to adjust the sizes of their pictures so that one unit in their picture corresponds to one unit on their adjustable grid. This is accomplished by resizing the pictures such that the unit marks on the ruler in each picture is equal to the length of one grid square. Once the pictures are properly superimposed over the grid, students can estimate the area of their leaves by counting the number of squares the image covers.

After students estimate the area of their leaves, they can check their estimations by using the calculation features of Sketchpad. To do this, students must plot points around the perimeter of the leaves. Once the points are plotted, the children can construct a polygon (and the polygon's interior) that models the shapes of their leaves. By measuring the area of their polygon's interior, students can calculate an approximate value for the area of their leaves (see Figure 4). Teachers can have students investigate how their approximations change as the number of points plotted around the perimeter increases.

Proportional Reasoning
Creating Contexts for Story Problems
GRADE LEVELS: 4–8

Objective

■ Students will develop and explore proportions in realistic settings.

NETS·S Addressed

1. Basic operations and concepts

- Students are proficient in the use of technology.

3. Technology productivity tools

- Students use technology tools to enhance learning, increase productivity, and promote creativity.

4. Technology communications tools

- Students use a variety of media and formats to communicate information and ideas effectively to multiple audiences.

5. Technology research tools

- Students use technology to locate, evaluate, and collect information from a variety of sources.

6. Technology problem-solving and decision-making tools

- Students use technology resources for solving problems and making informed decisions.

Mathematics Standards Addressed

Number and Operations Standard: Instructional programs from prekindergarten through Grade 12 should enable all students to:

- Understand numbers, ways of representing numbers, relationships among numbers, and number systems
- Compute fluently and make reasonable estimates

Problem Solving Standard: Instructional programs from prekindergarten through Grade 12 should enable all students to:

- Apply and adapt a variety of appropriate strategies to solve problems
- Monitor and reflect on the process of mathematical problem solving

Algebra Standard: Instructional programs from prekindergarten through Grade 12 should enable all students to:

- Use mathematical models to represent and understand quantitative relationships

Materials Needed

digital images of linear phenomena

dynamic geometry software such as the Geometer's Sketchpad (optional)

Activities

A SINGLE digital image can provide the context for a word problem that promotes the use of problem-solving skills. Consider the problem posed in Figure 5. The image and question in Figure 5 make up a contextual word problem.

ACQUIRE AND ANALYZE

For this problem, the picture is obviously a crucial element in the solution process. Unlike in the previous examples, the problem poser acquired this image himself. Although students may come up with a variety of solution methods, all the methods require some analysis of the picture. For example, some students may use the hypothesis that the paper posted on the wall beside Garrett is 11 inches long. Using this assumption, students could take measurements of the images of Garrett and the piece of paper (using Sketchpad or the line tool in programs like Word) and set up ratios that lead to an approximation of Garrett's height.

CREATE AND COMMUNICATE

Once students gain experience working with these types of word problems, they can create their own problems based on digital images that they acquire themselves. As part of the problem-solving experience, students will communicate their ideas about the role of the picture in the solution process, the accuracy of their results, and how digital images and proportional reasoning can be used to solve other applied measurement scenarios (for example, how a criminologist might use the video from a bank's security camera to determine a suspect's height).

FIGURE 5. How tall was Garrett at the time this picture was taken?

Photo by Brian Sharp.

Storm of the Century
Creating Contexts for Story Problems
GRADE LEVELS: 4–9

Objective

■ Students will develop problem-solving strategies and estimation skills in a realistic situation.

NETS•S Addressed

1. Basic operations and concepts

- Students are proficient in the use of technology.

3. Technology productivity tools

- Students use technology tools to enhance learning, increase productivity, and promote creativity.

4. Technology communications tools

- Students use a variety of media and formats to communicate information and ideas effectively to multiple audiences.

5. Technology research tools

- Students use technology to locate, evaluate, and collect information from a variety of sources.

6. Technology problem-solving and decision-making tools

- Students use technology resources for solving problems and making informed decisions.

Mathematics Standards Addressed

Number and Operations Standard: Instructional programs from prekindergarten through Grade 12 should enable all students to:

- Compute fluently and make reasonable estimates

Problem Solving Standard: Instructional programs from prekindergarten through Grade 12 should enable all students to:

- Apply and adapt a variety of appropriate strategies to solve problems
- Monitor and reflect on the process of mathematical problem solving

Algebra Standard: Instructional programs from prekindergarten through Grade 12 should enable all students to:

- Use mathematical models to represent and understand quantitative relationships

Materials Needed

digital images of realistic situations and phenomena

Activities

A SECOND, more complex example of a digital story problem comes from a personal experience. One of the authors of this chapter found herself in March 2003 stuck in the "snowstorm of the century" in the mountains of Colorado. Desiring to share this experience with her students, she decided to create a story problem using her digital camera. The story problem follows:

The Storm of the Century Problem

IN THE WINTER OF 2003, Ann, her husband, Bruce, and their golden retriever, Nedie, were snowed in for four days by a big storm in Colorado (Figures 6, 7, and 8). Bruce and Nedie spent quite a bit of time shoveling. Notice in Figure 6 that Bruce is walking on snowshoes.

They were afraid that their back deck would collapse under the weight of the snow, so they shoveled the snow on the deck regularly. The deck rails are 3.5 feet high and the snow on the deck rail is about 3 hours' worth. It snowed constantly for 56 hours.

Figure 9 shows Ann, on snowshoes, at the end of the storm. The decks are 4.5 feet off the ground.

PROBLEM: Using information from each of the pictures, make your best estimate of the amount of snow we received during the storm. Explain how each picture provided data for your estimation. Also indicate the lowest amount of snow you would estimate from the pictures and the highest, providing reasons for these answers.

This digital story problem allowed students to share in their teacher's adventure in the snow, while at the same time helping students to develop their estimation skills. Students can build similar story problems out of their own experiences using digital cameras. Working with this kind of material provides learners with a far more authentic and practical mathematics application than stories of boats traveling upstream or of ladders leaning against houses.

To be successful with this kind of activity, teachers need to provide clear, detailed instructions and a solid framework for building up the story elements. On the most general level, a mathematics digital story problem should contain the following elements:

- The story should present an authentic and interesting situation.

- The mathematics should be embedded in the story, rather than being the total focus of the story.

- The story should contain both relevant and irrelevant mathematical information.

Photo by Ann Thompson.

FIGURE 6. Bruce and Nedie in the snow.

Photo by Ann Thompson.

FIGURE 7. Nedie had a terrific time playing in the snow, but found it very deep at times.

Photo by Ann Thompson.

FIGURE 8. The back deck.

Photo by Bruce Thompson.

FIGURE 9. Ann on snowshoes.

- The story should contain a clear problem and directions for presenting a solution.

- Students should be encouraged to explain their problem-solving procedures; they can even be encouraged to use digital pictures to clarify their responses.

ACQUIRE

Students creating digital story problems will begin by capturing images from everyday life. Once several images have been acquired, students can organize these images into meaningful groups and sequences.

CREATE AND COMMUNICATE

When students have a good group of related images, they should add text and structure to create their story problems. Teachers and students can work together to find ways to communicate their work to appropriate audiences. These audiences might include peers, parents, younger students, or senior citizens. The communication phase of the project can provide rich possibilities for discussing and enjoying mathematics.

The Girl Who Loved Math
Digital Stories about Mathematics
GRADE LEVELS: K–8

Objective

■ Students will develop and explore mathematics in realistic settings.

NETS•S Addressed

1. Basic operations and concepts

- Students are proficient in the use of technology.

3. Technology productivity tools

- Students use technology tools to enhance learning, increase productivity, and promote creativity.

4. Technology communications tools

- Students use a variety of media and formats to communicate information and ideas effectively to multiple audiences.

Mathematics Standards Addressed

Number and Operations Standard: Instructional programs from prekindergarten through Grade 12 should enable all students to:

- Understand meanings of operations and how they relate to one another
- Compute fluently and make reasonable estimates

Connections Standard: Instructional programs from prekindergarten through Grade 12 should enable all students to:

- Recognize and apply mathematics in contexts outside of mathematics

Communication Standard: Instructional programs from prekindergarten through Grade 12 should enable all students to:

- Organize and consolidate their mathematical thinking through communication

Materials Needed

digital or drawn images of personal situations

Activities

THIS ACTIVITY is based on a story written by Ruby (daughter of one of the authors) in Ms. Messina's kindergarten class. She titled her story "The Girl Who Loved Math." In the story, Ruby tells of a girl named Mary who loved mathematics and cites examples that range from experiences in the grocery store to buying drinks at a basketball game. Ruby's entire story is available on the CD-ROM accompanying this book, but the following illustrations provide a sense of the content of this story.

For her book Ruby first recognized and *analyzed* instances of mathematics in her life. She then *created* or *acquired* images to illustrate these mathematical situations. Finally, she wrote her story to *communicate* some of her thinking about mathematics.

Ruby used a digital image (taken by her teacher) of herself working on her book for the inside cover of her book (see Figure 10).

She then used a combination of drawn and digital images to portray recent life experiences in which she recognized instances of the use of counting. See Figures 11 and 12.

Ruby's story provides a compelling example of the power of combining images and text for creating projects focused on mathematics in everyday life. Products like Ruby's story can be communicated with peers and parents to help stimulate thinking and conversation about mathematics in the world around us.

Both teachers and students will need a means to communicate their digital stories to other mathematics learners. Shared digital stories will provide students across the United States and the world with new, authentic mathematics experiences to explore and enjoy.

Ruby Garofalo
Red Hill Elementary School
Kindergarten
March 2003

Photo by Ann Messina, Albemarle County Schools.

FIGURE 10. The inside cover of Ruby's story book.

Mary went shopping with her mother. Mary bought ten packages of mushrooms. Ten mushrooms are in each package.
10 20 30 40 50
60 70 80 90 100.

Art by Ruby.

FIGURE 11. A drawn image in Ruby's book.

Mary went to the basketball game. She bought a 7up for$1. 96.

Photo by Ann Messina, Albemarle County Schools.

FIGURE 12. A digital image in Ruby's book.

Art by Ruby.

FIGURE 13. Basketball game image in Ruby's book.

Conclusion

IN THIS chapter we have provided several examples of how digital images can be incorporated into mathematics teaching. Our examples show how digital images can be used as an essential part of a lesson, rather than just "dressing up" the lesson with nice pictures. We believe that digital imagery can help students develop a keener sense of the reality of mathematics in the world around them. Because digital cameras are just now beginning to find their way into mathematics classrooms, much more needs to be done to determine all the different ways that digital cameras can promote the learning of mathematics.

Resources for More Information

National Council of Teachers of Mathematics. (2000). *Principles and standards for school mathematics.* Reston, VA: Author.

Sharp, B., Garofalo, J., & Thompson, A. (2004). Using digital images in mathematics teaching. *Learning and Leading with Technology, 31*(8), 30-32.

CHAPTER 9

*Michael J. Berson and
Kathleen Owings Swan*

digital images
in the social studies classroom

TODAY'S STUDENTS typically spend far more time looking at, thinking about, and engaged with images than they do static, printed text. Given the multimedia environment in which young people are immersed—television, movies, video games, Web pages, magazines—achieving success as a student and as a 21st century citizen necessitates that individuals "develop expertise with the increasingly sophisticated information and entertainment media that address us on a multisensory level, affecting the way we think, feel and behave" (Alliance for a Mediate Literate America, n.d.). Educators play an integral role in preparing students to use and make sense of these emerging media technologies.

Social studies teachers have responded to our overwhelmingly visual media environment by embracing instructional innovations that promote proficiency in analyzing images as representations of information. Creating and arranging pictures as artifacts within a digital space allow students to explore events from multiple perspectives. However, analyzing those images requires skills that must be developed with explicit instruction and practice. Deciding how to capture an image to accurately reflect the context of an event helps students to understand how pictures can serve as evidence of life at a particular historical point in time, and what those images say about the people living at that time. Such tasks actively prepare students with critical citizenship skills: observing primary sources, drawing conclusions, comparing findings, and interpreting the meaning of the depicted objects and activities.

These "digital literacy" skills (combining media literacy and visual literacy) are important foundations of historical inquiry. Activities that sensitize students to attend closely to data found in images can override their tendency to take all information at face value. Through this close reading and analysis of images, students can learn to construct richer meaning and understanding from diverse sources of information. Images depicting a particular place in the past and present or from a variety of perspectives can be compared to expand students' capacity for historical analysis. The two photos of Charleston, South Carolina, in Figure 1, for example, can be used to challenge students to distinguish and account for differences between Charleston, South Carolina, around 1865 and the same city in 2004.

Within the social studies, this process of accessing and interpreting information optimizes an individual's capacity for effective citizenship (Berson & Berson, 2003). Multimedia technology has enhanced access to diverse resources that enrich the learning experience and provide an opportunity for students not only to examine archives of visual information, but also to engage in authentic learning through the creation, analysis, and interpretation of digital images. This process enables students to explore patterns, manipulate information, discover connections, and synthesize resources in ways that transform their understanding of the material. What has often been overlooked in this process, however, is the necessary step of helping students to acquire the skills they need to evaluate the content, presentation, and value of the images they encounter. This component of instruction is addressed in digital literacy initiatives.

A notable connection between digital literacy and the social studies content standards is the promotion of citizenship skills within a global environment. As Kubey (2002, p. 1) notes, "media education is the entitlement of every citizen, in every country of the world, to freedom of expression and the right to information and is instrumental in building and sustaining a democracy." In the social studies, this literacy is necessary for an informed electorate that is knowledgeable about accessing credible information through communication technologies, and analyzing both the content of messages and their value for civic involvement.

Photo courtesy of the Library of Congress, Prints & Photographs Division, LC-DIG-cwpb-02355.

Photo © Ron Anton Rocz, RonRoczPhoto.com.

FIGURE 1. Charleston, South Carolina, past and present.

Promoting digital literacy is not an entirely new area of emphasis in the social studies, and several skills that are essential for evaluating images are already an integral component of social studies curricula. In an era of increasing educational accountability, new innovations in education must be linked to content standards in order to succeed. Current national standards in social studies lend themselves to working with images. The goal of digital literacy initiatives should be to enhance and enrich existing social studies curricula, building from a base of solid pedagogical practice. There are strong potential connections in all the areas of social science education.

All state and national educational standards have literacy at their core. At least 32 states in the U.S. have included skills in their state social studies frameworks that promote media literacy (Kubey & Baker, 1999). These include competencies in understanding perspective or point of view, developing critical thinking skills to analyze and evaluate the validity and credibility of information, accessing diverse forms of information, and working in digital environments.

Similarly, the national social studies standards designed by the National Council for the Social Studies (NCSS, 1994) promote literacy skills with performance expectations that include interpreting information, engaging in research with diverse resources, and constructing new representations of knowledge. A shared emphasis on critical thinking skills creates compatibility between media literacy and the existing social studies framework.

For example, the NCSS Science, Technology, and Society performance expectations for high schoolers note that learners should "recognize and interpret varied perspectives about human societies and the physical world using scientific knowledge, ethical standards, and technologies from diverse world cultures." This objective embraces the media literacy goals of accessing information, analyzing the meaning of messages, and making connections between an individual's values and diverse points of view.

Moreover, the NCSS theme of Time, Continuity, and Change includes experiences that "investigate, interpret, and analyze multiple historical and contemporary viewpoints within and across cultures related to important events, recurring dilemmas, and persistent issues, while employing empathy, skepticism, and critical judgment."

Digital literacy activities provide an almost limitless resource for exploring these skills, including opportunities to locate information from a variety of sources, consider how point of view is captured in a visual image, reflect on selection of the subject in a photograph, interpret the message being conveyed, and judge the veracity, quality, and relevance of the information. For the social studies, development of these skills formulates the necessary foundation for fulfilling one's role as a citizen in a democratic society.

Using Images to Promote Student Achievement

PRIMARY SOURCES have long been valued in social studies education as an instructional tool for teaching students content and processing skills. Primary sources are the records made by people who saw or took part in a particular historical event. These people may have written their thoughts in a journal, or they may have told their story in a letter or a poem. Alternatively, they may have made a speech, produced a film, taken a photograph, or painted a picture. Primary sources may also be objects or official documents that give information about the time in which they were made or written. A primary source gives people today a direct link to a past event.

A secondary source is not a direct link to a past event. It is a record of the event written by someone who was not there at the time. A magazine article, newspaper story, or book written by someone who only heard about or read about the event is a secondary source. So is an object made at a later time.

Some sources can be either primary or secondary, depending on how the event is reported. A newspaper might print the exact words of a person who saw the event take place. It might also print an article about the event, written by a reporter who was not there. Oral histories, textbooks, and online resources can also be either primary or secondary sources. (Berson, 2005, pp. 4-5)

Photographic images offer students the opportunity to engage personally and critically with primary and secondary sources, building their capacity to analyze and interpret historical information. This is an essential skill for functioning in today's society, where we are bombarded by an enticing amalgamation of images from many sources: mass media, the Web, books, films, a variety of digital technologies, family collections, and so on. The integration of digital photography into social studies instruction represents an authentic, hands-on, inquiry-based application of technology that prepares students with the skills necessary to access, analyze, and evaluate all forms of information and communication. Students learn to recognize how images can depict diverse perspectives, can connect disparate pieces of information, and can be manipulated to alter the authenticity or reliability of that information. Working with visual material fosters skills that are important when judging the accuracy and meaning of the evening news, museum displays, films, and other sources of information. The incorporation of images into instruction can also serve as a great motivator, as young people intrinsically enjoy working with images and engaging in the process of deducing what is happening in a picture.

CONTENT STANDARDS

The Social Studies Standards are sponsored by the National Council for the Social Studies, **www.ncss.org**.

By simulating the engagement of social scientists with primary and secondary sources, students can be challenged to evaluate information more critically. Designing technology-enhanced instructional activities is based on the recognition that real-world skills can be strengthened through engagement in simulated contexts. Student achievement as measured by the goals and objectives of social studies learning standards can be promoted through technology integration (Danker, 2000).

In the sections that follow, we detail three digital imaging projects that could be used to foster critical thinking and inquiry-based learning in the social studies classroom.

Spinning the News
Manipulating Imaging to Shape a Story
GRADE LEVELS: 6–8

Objectives

- Students will understand the process of decoding, evaluating, analyzing, and producing print and electronic media.

- Students will be able to create a news story from two different perspectives by manipulating digital images.

NETS•S Addressed

2. Social, ethical, and human issues

- Students understand the ethical, cultural, and societal issues related to technology.

3. Technology productivity tools

- Students use productivity tools to collaborate in constructing technology-enhanced models, preparing publications, and producing other creative works.

Social Studies Standards Addressed

Thematic Strand I: Culture

- Social studies programs should include experiences that provide for the study of culture and cultural diversity.

Materials Needed

access to classroom sets of two to four digital cameras

computers with access to the Internet

presentation software (iMovie, Movie Maker, or PowerPoint)

Web Resources

The Center for Media Literacy
www.medialit.org/focus/ss_home.html
   The Center for Media Literacy provides online resources for teaching media literacy in the social studies. This site offers various lesson plans and specific approaches to instruction.

The New York Times: Guidelines on Our Integrity
www.asne.org/index.cfm?id=408
   This Web site details the New York Times' position on preserving journalistic integrity, including the treatment of photographs.

Photo Forgery: Getting to the Heart of a Photojournalist's Code of Ethics
www.nytimes.com/learning/teachers/lessons/20040311thursday.html?search
   At this New York Times Learning Network site by Clayton DeKorne and Tanya Yasmin Chin, students can inspect examples of manipulated photos and learn about the technology and issues behind

"doctored" photos, leading to an in-depth discussion about the responsibility of the photojournalist and news editor to show "true" photos.

Project Look Sharp: Media Construction of War: A Critical Reading of History
http://gpn.unl.edu/cml/cml_series_product.asp?catalog%5Fname=GPN&category%5Fname= General+Audience+Media+Literacy&product%5Fid=1524
This is a multimedia curriculum kit designed by classroom social studies teachers at Project Look Sharp in Ithaca, New York. Students develop visual literacy and critical thinking skills while learning core historical information required by state and national social studies standards. They also learn to ask key media literacy questions, identify bias in the news, and gain the visual decoding skills needed to practice critical reading of historical documents and answer document-based questions (DBQs).

Activities

WITH THE advent of personal computers and image editing software programs such as Adobe Photoshop Elements, images can easily be altered after they are taken. The line between truth and fiction (always a difficult one to draw) has been further blurred for today's media consumer. Readers and viewers who look to mass media as their principal source of information about events occurring around the globe depend on journalists to represent those events with as much accuracy as possible. In the context of democracy, journalism is given a critical role: citizens obtain the information they need to become an informed body of voters through the work of journalists. If journalism loses the public's trust, it can derail the democratic process.

This activity is designed to facilitate deeper understanding of the role of the media and the importance of media literacy by making students aware of ways journalists can alter, distort, and exaggerate issues and events.

In recent years, photo manipulation has become both easy and pervasive. In 1982, the public was outraged to learn that *National Geographic* had digitally moved the pyramids in Egypt closer together to fit the magazine cover's vertical format. A similar stir occurred in June 1994 when a picture of O.J. Simpson appeared on the cover of *Time* magazine. For the cover, a Los Angeles police photo was electronically manipulated to create what *Time* called a "photo illustration." Some argued that the darkening of the photo made Simpson appear more sinister and thereby intentionally misled the public.

Today, this type of photo manipulation technology is available to anyone with a personal computer. It can even be found at the film development kiosks at local drug stores and supermarkets. People can go to these kiosks and develop their digital pictures using machines that can remove red eye, crop out unwanted details, and darken and lighten the image with the push of a button. However, while digital image editing software has allowed the art of photography to become ever more sophisticated and automated, it has also put the lie to the old cliché "The camera never lies." Perhaps the *camera* does not lie, but the photographer sure can, since the camera serves as both a literal and figurative perspective lens in which he or she frames an event. In fact, every choice a photographer makes in taking a picture involves subjectivity, from the camera angle (looking up, looking down, looking at eye level) to the framing (what to include and what to leave out) to the moment of exposure (when to shoot and when to wait).

As a result, it has become increasingly important for young consumers to become savvy consumers of media and understand the role of the media in shaping public opinion. This activity acquaints students with digital photography, photo manipulation, and journalistic bias. It puts students in the role of reporters who attempt to remove bias from a story and also deliberately manipulate a story to sway public opinion. Afterward, the students discuss the ethical dilemmas faced by journalists and readers. This introduction can serve as a jumping off point and a way to orient students to the issues that face journalists when telling a story.

ACQUIRE

In the first step of this activity, students are asked to report on an event or issue occurring at their school. Examples include a special event such as a basketball game, school dance, or charity drive; alternatively, students could report on an ongoing issue such as bullying, alcohol abuse among teens, or the pressure of college applications. Students become members of a newsroom in which groups work collaboratively on sections such as current events, sports, or entertainment. Acting as journalists, students collect information about the event or issue they are covering. This could include interviewing, observing, and using a digital camera to capture images that will illustrate the story.

CREATE

Students should then be given an opportunity to write two different versions of the same story. One story should limit as much as possible any inherent personal bias, while the other should make the most of the student's bias on the topic. For example, students can use image editing software to alter images in the second story by cropping the photo, changing the shading of the image, and perhaps removing persons or things from the image. They should also look for ways to use language differently to elicit a particular perspective or response. It is important that students understand that these articles are *not* opinion pieces; rather, they should both be presented as factual accounts of an event or issue. Language and photo manipulation should be used solely to exaggerate a point of view.

COMMUNICATE

Once students have completed their pieces, the class should work together to construct two newspapers, laying out the various sections using simple word processing software or (if available) publishing software. Although this activity can be done without the use of computers and digital images, it is important to note that this basic technology can enhance the appearance of the newspapers and the accompanying photographs. When used properly, altered images should appear believable.

ANALYZE

Students should be given time to read and enjoy the two newspapers, noting the differences and similarities between the two. As a class, students should then be encouraged to discuss the following questions:

- Is there an inherent bias in each of the newspapers? Provide examples.

- Does photography change the story? How?

- How can language be used to alter our understanding of an event? Are there specific instances in which the presentation attempts to sway readers by word choice or writing style?

- Should images be altered in the news? When is it appropriate to alter an image? Is photo manipulation ever justifiable?

- Some photographers argue that the phrase "manipulated photography" is a redundancy, since every photograph is manipulated. Is this true?

Finally, have students read the New York Times: Guidelines on Our Integrity (**www.asne. org/index.cfm?id=408**) and answer the following questions:

- How are journalistic ethics observed today?

- Where should the lines be drawn?

- Is there such a thing as unbiased reporting?

Becoming an informed member of the electorate is critical to full participation in society and is a central purpose of the social studies. By examining some of the issues surrounding media literacy, students can become more aware of the various partisanships and perspectives that influence them as voters, consumers, and citizens. The strategies presented offer an initial framework for realizing the potential of using imagery to teach emergent themes in the social studies and the larger social studies curriculum.

From Horses to Hondas
GRADE LEVELS: 5–8

Objectives

- Students will understand that the study of history involves a process of investigation, specifically reasoning using artifacts from the past.
- Students will be able to explain patterns of historical continuity and change over time by comparing archived images with their modern-day counterparts.

NETS·S Addressed

3. Technology productivity tools

- Students use productivity tools to collaborate in constructing technology-enhanced models, preparing publications, and producing other creative works.

5. Technology research tools

- Student use technology to locate, evaluate, and collect information from a variety of sources.

Social Studies Standards Addressed

Thematic Strand II: Time, Continuity, and Change

- Social studies programs should include experiences that provide for the study of the ways human beings view themselves in and over time.

Materials Needed

access to classroom sets of two to four digital cameras

computers with access to the Internet

presentation software (iMovie, Movie Maker, or PowerPoint)

Web Resources

The Historical Scene Investigation Project (HIS)
www.hsionline.org
    The Historical Scene Investigation Project was designed for social studies teachers who need a strong pedagogical mechanism for bringing primary sources into their classroom. The site includes a number of investigations, standardized as historic cases, for students to explore using primary sources. For every case, there is a section for the teacher. This section lists particular objectives for the activity and also provides additional contextual information and resources as well as instructional strategies that the teacher might find useful.

SCIM-C Historical Inquiry Tutorial
http://edpsychserver.ed.vt.edu/scim/soced/
    The SCIM-C Historical Inquiry Tutorial, a multimedia instructional scaffold, was designed as a freely accessible Web tool to assist teachers and students in developing an understanding of historical inquiry skills. The design of the SCIM-C tutorial is based on historical inquiry research, empirical guidelines for cognitive strategy instruction, empirical guidelines for instructional multimedia development, and transcripts of historians engaging in historical inquiry. Each instructional session comprises three sections: strategy explanation, strategy modeling, and strategy practice.

University of Virginia Special Collections Library, Holsinger Studio Collection
www.lib.virginia.edu/speccol/collections/holsinger/
> The Holsinger Studio Collection offers a photographic record of life in Charlottesville and Albemarle County, Virginia, from before the turn of the century through World War I.

U.S. National Archives and Records Administration
www.nara.gov
> The National Archives provides a range of U.S. history primary sources along with additional resources for teaching history in the social studies. Within this site are various lesson plans along with document analysis sheets as a means for deconstructing primary sources.

Activities

THE PURPOSE of teaching history is to provide students with the content knowledge, intellectual skills, and civic values necessary for fulfilling the role of citizen in a multi-cultural, participatory democracy. The authors of the National Standards for History (National Center for History in the Schools, 1994, p. 49), for example, argue that knowledge of history "is the precondition of political intelligence" and define history as "a process of reasoning based on evidence from the past" that "must be grounded in the careful gathering, weighing and sifting of factual information such as names, dates, places, ideas, and events."

According to these standards, historical thinking skills differ significantly from historical understandings. Historical understandings refer to content-specific knowledge. Historical thinking, on the other hand, encompasses the "doing of history": chronological thinking, historical comprehension, historical analysis and interpretation, historical research, historical issues analysis, and historical decision-making. Digital images hold the potential to facilitate these skills and understandings.

This project is designed to facilitate deeper student understanding of chronology and change over time using archived photographs and digital images. The National Standards for History emphasize the "importance of teaching students to identify the temporal sequence in which events occurred, to measure calendar time, to interpret and create timelines, and to explain patterns of historical continuity and change" (National Center for History in the Schools, 1994, p. 6). This introduction to chronological thinking could be used as a springboard for local history projects.

ACQUIRE

The University of Virginia Special Collections Library, like many libraries and museums, has established an online database of nearly 1,000 digitized historical images of the local community. The Holsinger Studio Collection (**www.lib.virginia.edu/speccol/collections/holsinger/**) offers a photographic record of life in central Virginia from the late 1800s through the 1920s. Teachers who wish to replicate this activity in their own community might find the local historical society to be a useful starting point. Local families and community founders are often willing to provide support for such efforts as well.

Students should be assigned to thematic groups, such as buildings, roads, people, commerce, culture, and transportation. Each group can assume responsibility for searching the database and acquiring at least three historic photographs that reflect their assigned theme. For example, students in the transportation or the building group might choose the photographs in Figures 2 and 3.

Students can be directed to save their images on a PC by right-clicking on the image and then saving it to a folder on their desktop.

ANALYZE

The Photo Analysis Worksheet in Table 1, developed by the National Archives and Records Administration, may be useful for the next stage of the activity. Students complete one worksheet per photograph.

TABLE 1. A Worksheet for Analyzing Historic Photographs

PHOTO ANALYSIS WORKSHEET

Adapted from the National Archives and Records Administration,
www.archives.gov/digital_classroom/lessons/analysis_worksheets/photo.html.

1. Observations

a. Study the photograph for two minutes. Form an overall impression of the photograph and then examine individual items. Next, divide the photo into quadrants and study each section to see what new details become visible.

b. List the people, objects, and activities in the photograph.

2. Inference

Based on what you have observed, list three things you might infer from the photograph.

3. Questions

a. What questions does this photograph raise in your mind?

b. Where could you find answers to them?

CREATE

Students should then be given an opportunity to capture equivalent modern-day scenes or subjects. For example, the pictures in Figures 4 and 5 are the 2005 version of the photographs in Figures 2 and 3.

In their thematic groups, students can be given a set of cameras to use for capturing their modern-day images. Students can also be provided with maps for locating where the archived image was originally taken. Each student in the group should capture at least one image to ensure full student participation, and parents should be notified so that they can facilitate the project.

COMMUNICATE

Once students have captured modern-day photographic equivalents, they can construct a visual historical narrative that examines the concept of change over time in relation to their chosen theme. Although this type of activity can be done using conventional film cameras, access to images in digital form facilitates a number of important steps in the

© Holsinger Studio Collection (#9862), special collections, University of Virginia Library.

FIGURE 2. 17 University Circle, 1914.

activity. Students can, of course, incorporate digital images into other digital files such as Word documents and PowerPoint presentations.

Students can also develop short digital stories in the style pioneered by filmmaker Ken Burns, combining still images with an accompanying audio narrative to create a short digital film. While this type of activity was once the province of professional documentary makers, the advent of free (or very affordable) nonlinear digital video editors such as Movie Maker and iMovie now brings this capability into today's classrooms. Comparable activities can be undertaken on older computers through presentation programs such as PowerPoint.

Provide students who are creating this kind of documentary film with the following guidelines for their narration:

- Describe each photograph.

- Describe the process of historical excavation required to locate and capture the modern-day image.

- What has happened since the original photograph was taken? How do you know?

© Holsinger Studio Collection (#9862), special collections, University of Virginia Library.

FIGURE 3. Main Street, 1917.

Photo by Lynn Bell.

FIGURE 4. 17 University Circle, 2005.

Photo by Lynn Bell.

FIGURE 5. Main Street, 2005.

- What more would you like to know about each photograph? How would you find this out?

It is important to limit the scope of such projects. A digital movie of 90 seconds to three minutes is appropriate. A full-length documentary may take hundreds of professionals more than a year to produce. By limiting the scale to short vignettes, such projects can be realistic for classrooms.

In this example, the underlying historical concept of change over time can be used to frame discussions of the end products developed. Sharing these products with an audience—classmates, other classes, and parents—has proven to be an important part of the process in pilot efforts.

Historical thinking asks students to become detectives in the quest to make meaning of the past. These types of exercises actively engage students in uncovering past events, places, and people, and help social studies teachers in making history come alive and more relevant for their students. The strategies presented offer an initial framework for realizing the potential of digital imagery in history and the larger social studies curriculum.

Capturing and Identifying Geographic Features

GRADE LEVELS: 3–4

Objectives

- Students will collect or capture digital images representing landforms and water features in their community or throughout the world.

- Students will identify and label geographic features depicted in digital images.

NETS·S Addressed

3. Technology productivity tools

- Students use productivity tools to collaborate in constructing technology-enhanced models, preparing publications, and producing other creative works.

5. Technology research tools

- Student use technology to locate, evaluate, and collect information from a variety of sources.

Social Studies Standards Addressed

Thematic Strand III: People, Places, and Environments

- Social studies programs should include experiences that provide for the study of people, places, and environments.

Materials Needed

computers with Internet access

digital cameras (if students will be capturing images in their community)

software with editing capabilities (imageblender, Photoshop Elements, PowerPoint, or Microsoft Word)

Web Resources

CIA Factbook
www.odci.gov/cia/publications/factbook/index.html
    CIA Factbook offers a factually accurate listing of data by country that is updated in real time. It includes categories such as maps, transportation, people, government, economy, communications, and transnational issues.

Explore the Globe Program
www.globe.gov/fsl/welcome.html
    This site is ideal for elementary-level teachers who have a strong interest in active learning approaches. In addition to interactive activities for students, educators can access a teacher's guide, a data archive, and an image gallery.

Harcourt School Publishers
www.harcourtschool.com/glossary/horizons/index.html
    This site provide a glossary of geography terms.

National Atlas of the United States

www.nationalatlas.gov

> This site, developed by the U.S. Geological Survey, creates an atlas of U.S. natural and social-cultural landscapes. Interactive multimedia maps aid in the visualization and comprehension of complex relationships among places, people, and environments.

National Geographic Society

www.nationalgeographic.com

> This Web site provides access to the world of geography. Xpeditions provides more than 600 printable maps for use in the classroom and a variety of activities and information that enhance geography education.

Rubistar

http://rubistar.4teachers.org/index.php

> Rubistar is a free rubric making tool.

United States Geological Survey

http://mapping.usgs.gov/

> This site offers comprehensive lesson plans for different grade levels. The Land and People section includes global change and other contemporary topics. Information that allows integration of science and social studies is prevalent.

50 States and Capitals

www.50states.com

> This site provides easy access to statistical and historical information for each of the 50 states.

Activities

ELEMENTARY STUDENTS who study geography have the challenging task of learning about numerous geographic features all over the world (see Figure 6). Teachers have tried a number of strategies to teach geographic concepts with varying success. Some teachers have their students draw pictures of features, such as hills and mountains. The problem with this approach is that students sometimes lack the artistic skills to draw pictures that actually differentiate between the various landforms or water features.

The introduction of geographic images into instruction can enhance the teaching and learning process by providing concrete representations of concepts. The integration of visual cues with descriptive information can clarify unfamiliar terms and provide links to pre-existing knowledge about landforms and water features in the students' local environment. This process contributes to the necessary association between the understanding of geographic concepts and applied learning for use in everyday interactions.

ACQUIRE

This activity provides students an opportunity to focus on geographic features unique to their local setting or extend their study to landforms and water features in other regions. Students may be assigned a specific geographic feature to capture in a photo, such as finding an example of an estuary in their area, or they may take turns photographing several different landmarks and water features (such as mountains, lakes, or oceans) that they might see on a field trip in the community. Students also may seek out images

Photo by Lynn Bell.

FIGURE 6. Natural Bridge in Virginia.

online from sources such as National Geographic (**www.nationalgeographic.com**) and download them for later analysis. If students are focusing on one kind of geographic element, the online resources may provide varied representations of the highlighted feature. For example, images of a local estuary may be compared with photos of other estuaries found around the world, including Rio de la Plata, Gulf of Nicoya, Heuningnes estuary, and Milford Sound. Online resources also provide access to photos capturing a variety of geographic elements, and these images can be analyzed to determine which features are depicted.

ANALYZE

In this step, students import their photos into editing software, such as Microsoft Word, PowerPoint, imageblender, or Photoshop Elements. The task is to identify all the geographic features they observe in the digital images they have collected. These may include a butte, cliff, cape, canyon, continent, ocean, geyser, mesa, mountain, river, and so on. Geography textbooks and online resources such as Harcourt School Publishers

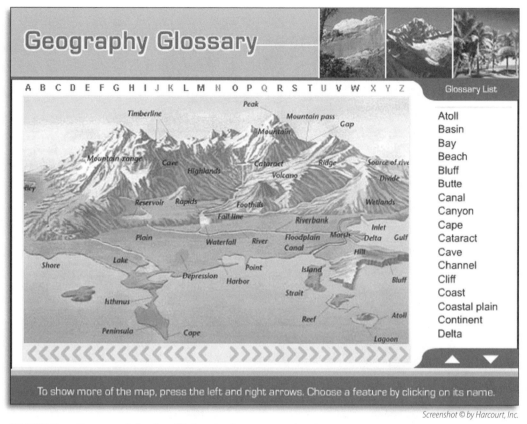

Screenshot © by Harcourt, Inc.

FIGURE 7. Harcourt School Publishers' online geography glossary.

(www.harcourtschool.com/glossary/horizons/) often provide a glossary of geography terms that can serve as a guide for students (Figure 7).

CREATE

Using the list of identified features, students should create labeled images, embedding the names of each geographic element in the photo with a paint program or word processing tool. Students may either develop a portfolio of diverse examples of a single geographic feature (for example, the mountains in Figure 8), or comprehensively identify the geographic landforms in one particular image (for example, the landscape in Figure 9).

COMMUNICATE

Students may integrate their labeled images into a PowerPoint presentation, Word document, or scrapbook (as in Figure 10) to show representative images of geographic features. A rubric developed with Rubistar (a free rubric making tool available at **http://rubistar.4teachers.org**), such as the example provided in Table 2, may be used to evaluate the students' final product.

Photo by Lynn Bell.

Photo by Randy L. Bell.

FIGURE 8. At top is the Abert Rim, one of the impressive fault scarps of Oregon. Below is Mount Jefferson, the second highest peak in the Oregon Cascade Range.

The ease of acquiring digital images from the Web and from students' digital photos has removed much of the challenge that elementary students formerly faced in learning about geographic features. The virtually unlimited supply of landscape images on the Web can help students develop clearer conceptions of basic landforms that can later be applied to map interpretation and other geography topics.

Conclusion

DIGITAL IMAGERY offers an enhanced way to explore the reality of American society through students' actual, lived experiences. Students who engage in active learning have personal, authentic experiences that strengthen their understanding of the given topic. Active learning is advanced when students are placed in control of their learning experience and contribute to the design of their own learning environment. The constructivist approach to learning embedded in the three projects described in this chapter encourages student activity, motivation, and authenticity in learning experiences (White, 1996). Our hope is that this chapter will begin a conversation about the potential for using digital images across the social studies disciplines.

Students can use digital cameras to capture images within their community to enhance their interpretation of local history, economics, geography, and politics. Students can also exchange their collected digital images electronically with classes in other locations, comparing them to foster the process of historical inquiry and interpretation across geographic regions. Digital camera technology has crossed an important

Photo by Lynn Bell.

FIGURE 9. Students can label the geographic features of a landscape.

Photo by Michael J. Berson.

FIGURE 10. A scrapbook of geographic locations.

threshold of cost and ease of use, making it suitable for wide scale application in schools. By facilitating inquiry-based learning, encouraging constructivist pedagogies, and disseminating an exchange of knowledge representations within a geographic locale, the classroom becomes a site of active learning and thinking, fostered by the technological resources available.

Resources for More Information

Alliance for a Mediate Literate America. (n.d.). *What is media literacy?* Retrieved November 8, 2004, from **www.amlainfo.org/medialit/index.php**

Berson, I. R., & Berson, M. J. (2003). Digital literacy for cybersafety, digital awareness, and media literacy. *Social Education, 67*(3), 164-168.

Berson, M. J. (Ed.). (2005). *Harcourt horizons: United States history.* Orlando, FL: Harcourt.

Danker, A. (2000). Linking technology with social studies learning standards. *The Social Studies, 91*(6), 253-256.

Kubey, R. (2002). How media education promotes critical thinking: Democracy, health, and aesthetic appreciation. In *Thinking critically about media: Schools and families in partnership.* Retrieved December 1, 2004, from **www.ciconline.com/Enrichment/ThinkingCritically/default.htm**

TABLE 2. Geography Project Rubric

	EXEMPLARY 4	PROFICIENT 3	SATISFACTORY 2	UNSATISFACTORY 1
ATTRACTIVENEESS	Makes excellent use of font, color, graphics, effects, etc. to enhance the presentation content.	Makes good use of font, color, graphics, effects, etc. to enhance the presentation content.	Makes use of font, color, graphics, effects, etc. but occasionally these detract from the presentation content.	Makes use of font, color, graphics, effects, etc. but these often detract from the presentation content.
CONTENT	Covers topics in-depth with details and examples. Subject knowledge is excellent.	Includes essential knowledge about the topic. Subject knowledge appears to be good.	Includes essential information about the topic but there are one or two factual errors.	Content is minimal OR there are several factual errors.
ORAL PRESENTATION	Interesting, well-rehearsed with smooth delivery that holds audience attention.	Relatively interesting, rehearsed with a fairly smooth delivery that usually holds audience attention.	Delivery not smooth, but able to hold audience attention most of the time.	Delivery not smooth and audience attention is often lost.
ORIGINALITY	Product shows a large amount of original thought. Ideas are creative and inventive.	Product shows some original thought. Work shows new ideas and insights.	Uses other people's ideas (giving them credit), but there is little evidence of original thinking.	Uses other people's ideas, but does not give them credit.
MECHANICS	No errors in spelling or grammar.	One to two errors in spelling or grammar.	Three to four errors in spelling or grammar.	More than four errors in spelling or grammar.
SOURCES	Source information collected for all graphics, facts, and quotes. All documented in desired format.	Source information collected for all graphics, facts, and quotes. Most documented in desired format.	Source information collected for all graphics, facts, and quotes, but not documented in desired format.	Very little or no source information was collected.

Kubey, R., & Baker, F. (1999, October). Has media literacy found a curricular foothold? *Education Week, 19*(9), 56.

National Center for History in the Schools. (1994). *National standards for United States history: Exploring the American experience.* Los Angeles: Author.

National Council for the Social Studies. (1994). *Expectations of excellence: Curriculum standards for social studies.* Washington, DC: Author.

White, C. (1996). Relevant social studies education: Integrating technology and constructivism. *Journal of Technology and Teacher Education, 4*(1), 69-76.

image resources
on the Web

THIS BOOK is the collective work of a group of educators who anticipate that the widespread diffusion of digital cameras throughout society will offer new educational possibilities. Digital cameras have become as ubiquitous as cell phones—and, as a result, an unprecedented number of digital images are being taken every day. This has given rise to numerous photo-sharing sites where digital images are posted and shared. Many of these sites allow images to be used freely for educational purposes.

Flikr (**www.flikr.com**) is one of the better-known photo-sharing sites, and is representative of these services. Flikr offers an application interface (API) to third-party developers that allows them to create applications that make use of Flikr images. Users can enter tags that can be searched using a third-party tag browser such as the following: **www.airtightinteractive.com/projects/related_tag_browser/app/**

A word tool (**http://metaatem.net/words/**) developed for Flikr allows students to enter words that are spelled out using letters drawn from the image collection (see Figure 1).

Another tool, Mappr (**www.mappr.com**), allows users to search on a tag and see a geographic distribution of images that have been photographed by Flikr users. For example, students in a botany class might click on the name of a plant such as "oak" and see an array of images of oaks taken in sites across the U.S. (see Figure 2).

Photographs uploaded to Flikr can be tagged with a Creative Commons license that permits educational sharing. Yahoo! recently announced the launching of a Creative Commons search engine (see **http://search.yahoo.com/cc**) that permits users to search the entire Web, filtering results on the basis of Creative Commons licenses.

Product © Ludicorp.

FIGURE 1. With the Flickr word tool, students can spell out words with images.

Product © Ludicorp.

FIGURE 2. The Mappr tool at Flickr allows users to see a geographic distribution of images taken by users.

Although it is currently in its beta version, this search engine promises to be a useful tool for educators and students looking for images to use in learning projects.

To ensure compliance with copyright law, you can take advantage of a number of other Web sites that specifically allow use of images for educational purposes. A sample of sites that were available at the time of publication are listed in the following sections. This is a fast-moving area of Internet innovation, so this list is subject to change.

History and Geography Image Collections

National Geographic
www.nationalgeographic.com/onestop
  On National Geographic's One-Stop Research page, search for maps, pictures, articles, video, and more by topic.

U.S. Library of Congress Prints and Photographs Reading Room
www.loc.gov/rr/print/catalog.html
  This is a searchable database of historic photographs, many of which are in the public domain.

U.S. National Archives and Records Administration (NARA)
www.archives.gov
  The mission of the NARA is to ensure ready access to the essential evidence that documents the rights of American citizens, the actions of federal officials, and the national experience.

Virginia Center for Digital History
www.vcdh.virginia.edu/research.html
> This site includes images related to the following American history topics (as well as other subjects):

- Civil War: **http://valley.vcdh.virginia.edu/Images/search_images.html**
- Jamestown, Virginia: **www.virtualjamestown.org/gallery.html**
- Dolley Madison: **www.vcdh.virginia.edu/madison/exhibit/index.html**
- Television News of the Civil Rights Era, 1950–1970: **www.vcdh.virginia.edu/civilrightstv**

Science Image Collections

Crocodilian Photo Gallery
www.flmnh.ufl.edu/herpetology/crocs/crocpics.htm
> This site hosts more than 120 photographs of alligators, caimans, crocodiles, and gharials.

Fossil Image Galleries, The Virtual Fossil Museum
www.fossilmuseum.net/index.htm
> This site offers picture galleries of fossils organized by taxonomy and fossil site. The policy for downloading these photos for educational use is not stated on the site, but the fossil images may be displayed for the class with a computer projector. Find more fossil images at the Fossil Images Archive, www.fossilmuseum.net/Education.htm

Hubble Site Gallery
http://hubblesite.org/gallery/
> The official site of the Hubble Space Telescope includes images of deep space objects and space shuttles.

Iowa State University Entomology Image Gallery
www.ent.iastate.edu/imagegallery/
> This site provides images of beetles, butterflies, mosquitoes, bugs, and more. Iowa State's image use policy can be found at www.ent.iastate.edu/legal/default.html

National Space Science Data Center Photo Gallery
http://nssdc.gsfc.nasa.gov/photo_gallery/photogallery-spacecraft.html
> This site hosts images of various NASA and other agency spacecraft.

Science Image
www.scienceimage.csiro.au/index.cfm?event=site.home
> This image library specializing in science and nature images provides licensing for schools.

Sonoran Desert JPEGS
www.miragemall.com/desertjpegs/imagesf.htm
> Go here for numerous photos of desert plants and animals.

General Image Collections

FreePhoto.com
www.freefoto.com
> At this site, 64,582 images are organized into 116 sections and 2,307 categories. The site's educational use policy can be found at www.freefoto.com/browse.jsp?id=99-16-0

FreeStockPhotos.com
http://freestockphotos.com/
> This site offers images of animals, weather, scenery, plants, and wildflowers.

Landscape Architecture Image Resource
www.lair.umd.edu
> This database provides photographs of countries, places, and architecture.

The Manzanita Project, Special Collections, California Academy of Sciences Library
www.calacademy.org/research/library/manzanita/html/images.html
> The image categories here include plants, fungi, animals, landscape and habitat, and people and culture. The site's educational use policy is at www.calacademy.org/research/library/manzanita/html/useinfo.htm#educational

The Morgue File
www.morguefile.com
> A morgue file is an archive of newspaper articles and photographs. This site offers archives of images contributed by users that are freely available for use without charge.

Open Photo
http://openphoto.net
> This site hosts a database of images covered by the Creative Commons license, which in general specifies that the works may be copied and distributed noncommercially, provided credit is given to the original author. Specific licensing terms may vary for individual photos, and these terms are clearly identified on the Web site.

Pics4Learning
www.pics4learning.com
> Pics4Learning is a copyright-friendly image library for teachers and students. The Pics4Learning collection consists of thousands of images that have been donated by students, teachers, and amateur photographers.

Ray I. Doan Photographic Collection
www.raydoan.com
> More than 700 professionally photographed landscape and wildlife images are offered here. Printed or high resolution images are available for a significant fee, but the photographer allows free downloads of the Web images for educational use. The site's educational use policy is at www.raydoan.com/Educational_Use.htm

The Stock Exchange
http://sxc.hu/
> The stock exchange is a collection of photographs contributed by amateur photographers who offer their work for use by the public without charge. The archive has more than 100,000 images arranged by categories such as nature, art and architecture, travel, and transportation.

National Educational Technology Standards for Students (NETS·S)

THE NATIONAL Educational Technology Standards for Students are divided into six broad categories. Standards within each category are to be introduced, reinforced, and mastered by students. Teachers can use these standards as guidelines for planning technology-based activities in which students achieve success in learning, communication, and life skills.

1. Basic operations and concepts

   - Students demonstrate a sound understanding of the nature and operation of technology systems.

   - Students are proficient in the use of technology.

2. Social, ethical, and human issues

   - Students understand the ethical, cultural, and societal issues related to technology.

   - Students practice responsible use of technology systems, information, and software.

   - Students develop positive attitudes toward technology uses that support lifelong learning, collaboration, personal pursuits, and productivity.

3. Technology productivity tools

   - Students use technology tools to enhance learning, increase productivity, and promote creativity.

   - Students use productivity tools to collaborate in constructing technology-enhanced models, preparing publications, and producing other creative works.

4. Technology communications tools

   - Students use telecommunications to collaborate, publish, and interact with peers, experts, and other audiences.

   - Students use a variety of media and formats to communicate information and ideas effectively to multiple audiences.

5. Technology research tools

   - Students use technology to locate, evaluate, and collect information from a variety of sources.

   - Students use technology tools to process data and report results.

   - Students evaluate and select new information resources and technological innovations based on the appropriateness to specific tasks.

6. Technology problem-solving and decision-making tools

   - Students use technology resources for solving problems and making informed decisions.

   - Students employ technology in the development of strategies for solving problems in the real world.

APPENDIX C

National Educational Technology Standards for Teachers
(NETS·T)

ALL CLASSROOM teachers should be prepared to meet the following standards and performance indicators.

I. Technology Operations and Concepts

Teachers demonstrate a sound understanding of technology operations and concepts. Teachers:

A. demonstrate introductory knowledge, skills, and understanding of concepts related to technology (as described in the ISTE National Educational Technology Standards for Students).

B. demonstrate continual growth in technology knowledge and skills to stay abreast of current and emerging technologies.

II. Planning and Designing Learning Environments and Experiences

Teachers plan and design effective learning environments and experiences supported by technology. Teachers:

A. design developmentally appropriate learning opportunities that apply technology-enhanced instructional strategies to support the diverse needs of learners.

B. apply current research on teaching and learning with technology when planning learning environments and experiences.

C. identify and locate technology resources and evaluate them for accuracy and suitability.

D. plan for the management of technology resources within the context of learning activities.

E. plan strategies to manage student learning in a technology-enhanced environment.

III. Teaching, Learning, and the Curriculum

Teachers implement curriculum plans that include methods and strategies for applying technology to maximize student learning. Teachers:

A. facilitate technology-enhanced experiences that address content standards and student technology standards.

B. use technology to support learner-centered strategies that address the diverse needs of students.

C. apply technology to develop students' higher-order skills and creativity.

D. manage student learning activities in a technology-enhanced environment.

IV. Assessment and Evaluation

Teachers apply technology to facilitate a variety of effective assessment and evaluation strategies. Teachers:

A. apply technology in assessing student learning of subject matter using a variety of assessment techniques.

B. use technology resources to collect and analyze data, interpret results, and communicate findings to improve instructional practice and maximize student learning.

C. apply multiple methods of evaluation to determine students' appropriate use of technology resources for learning, communication, and productivity.

V. Productivity and Professional Practice

Teachers use technology to enhance their productivity and professional practice. Teachers:

A. use technology resources to engage in ongoing professional development and lifelong learning.

B. continually evaluate and reflect on professional practice to make informed decisions regarding the use of technology in support of student learning.

C. apply technology to increase productivity.

D. use technology to communicate and collaborate with peers, parents, and the larger community in order to nurture student learning.

VI. Social, Ethical, Legal, and Human Issues

Teachers understand the social, ethical, legal, and human issues surrounding the use of technology in PK–12 schools and apply that understanding in practice. Teachers:

A. model and teach legal and ethical practice related to technology use.

B. apply technology resources to enable and empower learners with diverse backgrounds, characteristics, and abilities.

C. identify and use technology resources that affirm diversity.

D. promote safe and healthy use of technology resources.

E. facilitate equitable access to technology resources for all students.